Math Contests
for
Grades 4, 5, and 6
Volume 5

School Years
2001-2002 through 2005-2006

Written by

Steven R. Conrad • Daniel Flegler

Published by MATH LEAGUE PRESS
Printed in the United States of America

Cover art by Bob DeRosa

Phil Frank Cartoons Copyright © 1993 by CMS

First Printing, 2006

Copyright © 2006
by Mathematics Leagues Inc.
All Rights Reserved

Math League Press
P.O. Box 17
Tenafly, NJ 07670-0017

ISBN 0-940805-15-4

Preface

Math Contests—Grades 4, 5, and 6, Volume 5 is the fifth volume in our series of problem books for grades 4, 5, and 6. The first four volumes contain the contests given in the school years 1979-1980 through 2000-2001. This volume contains contests given from 2001-2002 through 2005-2006. (You can use the order form on page 154 to order any of our 15 books.)

This book is divided into three sections for ease of use by students and teachers. You'll find the contests in the first section. Each contest consists of 30 or 40 multiple-choice questions that you can do in 30 minutes. On each 3-page contest, the questions on the 1st page are generally straightforward, those on the 2nd page are moderate in difficulty, and those on the 3rd page are more difficult. In the second section of the book, you'll find detailed solutions to all the contest questions. In the third and final section of the book are the letter answers to each contest. In this section, you'll also find rating scales you can use to rate your performance.

Many people prefer to consult the answer section rather than the solution section when first reviewing a contest. We believe that reworking a problem when you know the answer (but *not* the solution) often leads to increased understanding of problem-solving techniques.

Each year we sponsor an Annual 4th Grade Mathematics Contest, an Annual 5th Grade Mathematics Contest, and an Annual 6th Grade Mathematics Contest. A student may participate in the contest on grade level or for any higher grade level. For example, students in grades 4 and 5 (or below) may participate in the 6th Grade Contest. Starting with the 1991-92 school year, students have been permitted to use calculators on any of our contests.

Steven R. Conrad & Daniel Flegler, contest authors

Acknowledgments

For demonstrating the meaning of selflessness on a daily basis, special thanks to Grace Flegler.

To Mark Motyka, we offer our gratitude for his assistance over the years.

To Jeannine Kolbush, who did an awesome proofreading job, thanks!

Table Of Contents

Preface i

Acknowledgements ii

Grade	School Year	Page for Contest	Page for Solutions	Page for Answers
4	2001-02	5	73	138
4	2002-03	9	77	139
4	2003-04	13	81	140
4	2004-05	17	85	141
4	2005-06	21	89	142
5	2001-02	27	95	143
5	2002-03	31	99	144
5	2003-04	35	103	145
5	2004-05	39	107	146
5	2005-06	43	111	147
6	2001-02	49	117	148
6	2002-03	53	121	149
6	2003-04	57	125	150
6	2004-05	61	129	151
6	2005-06	65	133	152

Order Form For Contest Books (Grades 4-12) 154

The Contests

. . . .

2001-2002 through 2005-2006

4th Grade Contests

2001-2002 through 2005-2006

2001-2002 Annual 4th Grade Contest

Spring, 2002

Instructions

4

- **Time** You will have only *30 minutes* working time for this contest. You might be *unable* to finish all 30 questions in the time allowed.

- **Scores** Please remember that *this is a contest, not a test*—and there is no "passing" or "failing" score. Few students score as high as 24 points (80% correct). Students with half that, 12 points, *deserve commendation!*

- **Format and Point Value** This is a multiple-choice contest. Each answer is an A, B, C, or D. Write each answer in the *Answer Column* to the right of each question. A correct answer is worth 1 point. Unanswered questions get no credit. You **may** use a calculator.

1. $20 \times 0 \times 2 =$

    A) 0   B) 40   C) 400   D) 2002

    1.

2. What is 3 more than 5 more than 7?

    A) 8   B) 10   C) 12   D) 15

    2.

3. We toasted 8 dozen marshmallows at our camp-fire. How many marshmallows did we toast?

    A) 12   B) 20   C) 64   D) 96

    3.

4. $9 - 8 + 7 - 6 + 5 - 4 + 3 - 2 = 1 + \underline{?}$

    A) 3   B) 4   C) 5   D) 8

    4.

5. If I had 9¢ more, I'd have $1. How much money do I have?

    A) 90¢   B) 91¢   C) 99¢   D) $1.09

    5.

6. If a flowering plant blooms for exacty 3 months each year, that same plant does *not* bloom for exactly $\underline{?}$ months each year.

    A) 3   B) 6   C) 9   D) 12

    6.

7. $1 + 1 + 10 + 10 + 100 + 100 = 111 + \underline{?}$

    A) 89   B) 99   C) 111   D) 121

    7.

8. Standing under a pear tree were the following birds: 4 calling birds, 3 French hens, 2 turtle doves, and 1 partridge. How many birds were standing under the pear tree?

    A) 9   B) 10   C) 11   D) 24

    8.

9. I got my immunization shot 6 days after Tuesday. The day was

    A) Sat.   B) Sun.   C) Mon.   D) Wed.

    9.

10. The sum of four 5s is

    A) $4 + 5$ B) 4×5 C) 45   D) 5555

    10.

11. Which of the following products does *not* equal 12×12?

    A) 3×48 B) 4×36 C) 6×24 D) 8×16

    11.

Go on to the next page ▌▌▌➡ **4**

12. What season is it two seasons before winter?

    A) winter   B) spring   C) autumn   D) summer

13. In 12 years, Ali will be twice as old as she is now. How old was Ali 4 years ago?

    A) 8   B) 16   C) 20   D) 28

14. $22 + 22 + 22 = 33 + 33 + 33 - \underline{\ ?\ }$

    A) 11   B) 22   C) 33   D) 66

15. How many whole numbers less than 100 are 2-digit numbers?

    A) 88   B) 89   C) 90   D) 91

16. Of four coins I got from a local store, one was equal in value to the sum of the other three. The total value of all four coins was

    A) 20¢   B) 25¢   C) 40¢   D) 50¢

17. What is the remainder when $(12 + 24 + 37)$ is divided by 12?

    A) 0   B) 1   C) 5   D) 9

18. Of the 18 fish in my aquarium, twice as many have stripes as do not have stripes. How many of my fish have stripes?

    A) 6   B) 9   C) 12   D) 15

19. When $\underline{\ ?\ }$ is divided by 99, the quotient is 11.

    A) 9   B) 88   C) 999   D) 1089

20. The sum of a whole number and 2 is *always* divisible by

    A) 0   B) 1   C) 2   D) 3

21. What time is it 11 hours and 11 minutes after 11:11 P.M.?

    A) 10:22 A.M.   B) 12 P.M.   C) 12 A.M.   D) 12:22 A.M.

22. If you write our alphabet alphabetically, how many letters do you write after the first vowel but before the last consonant?

    A) 23   B) 24   C) 25   D) 26

Go on to the next page ⟿ **4**

7

23. The number 246 858 642 is *not* divisible by

    A) 2   B) 4   C) 6   D) 9

    23.

24. What is the least possible difference between two whole numbers whose product is 124?

    A) 27   B) 31   C) 60   D) 123

    24.

25. At a charity car wash, each car wash cost the same amount. The total collected was $60. The cost of each car wash could *not* have been

    A) $9   B) $12   C) $30   D) 50¢

    25.

26. Without overlapping any two circles, I can fit at most ? circles with radius 2 inside a square with side-length 12.

    A) 6   B) 9   C) 12   D) 36

    26.

27. A delivery truck carries 8 cases. Each case contains 7 cartons. In each carton are 6 boxes. If each box contains 1 pie, exactly how many pies are in the 8 cases?

    A) 21   B) 62   C) 104   D) 336

    27.

28. If $2+4+6+ \ldots +48+50 = 650$, then $1+3+5+ \ldots +47+49 =$

    A) 599   B) 600   C) 625   D) 650

    28.

29. Twelve squares, each with side-length 2, are put together, without overlapping, to form a rectangle. What is the greatest possible perimeter of this rectangle?

    A) 28   B) 32   C) 52   D) 72

    29.

30. As the hour hand goes completely around the face of a circular clock one time, the minute hand goes completely around the face of the clock ? times.

    A) 12   B) 24   C) 60   D) 720

    30.

The end of the contest **4**

Visit our Web site at http://www.mathleague.com

Solutions on Page 73 • Answers on Page 138

2002-2003 Annual 4th Grade Contest

Spring, 2003

Instructions

4

- **Time** You will have only *30 minutes* working time for this contest. You might be *unable* to finish all 30 questions in the time allowed.

- **Scores** Please remember that *this is a contest, not a test*—and there is no "passing" or "failing" score. Few students score as high as 24 points (80% correct). Students with half that, 12 points, *deserve commendation!*

- **Format and Point Value** This is a multiple-choice contest. Each answer is an A, B, C, or D. Write each answer in the *Answer Column* to the right of each question. A correct answer is worth 1 point. Unanswered questions get no credit. You **may** use a calculator.

1. $2 \times 0 \times 0 \times 3 =$

   A) 0   B) 5   C) 6   D) 600

   1.

2. 8 more than 9 equals 10 more than

   A) 7   B) 8   C) 11   D) 19

   2.

3. $80 - 70 + 60 - 50 + 40 - 30 + 20 - 10 =$

   A) 10   B) 20   C) 30   D) 40

   3.

4. Each of the following is a prime number *except*

   A) 2   B) 3   C) 4   D) 5

   4.

5. I own 1 Minifish and 2 Giantfish. Each Giantfish weighs 3 times as much as my Minifish. If my Minifish eats my 2 Giantfish, my Minifish will eat _?_ times its own weight.

   A) 2   B) 3   C) 5   D) 6

   5.

6. My bank gave me 10 dimes and _?_ nickels for my 5 quarters.

   A) 5   B) 10   C) 15   D) 20

   6.

7. (number of hours in a day) ÷ (number of months in a year) =

   A) 2   B) 6   C) 12   D) 36

   7.

8. If each of my Bear Babies weighs 15 kg, then 5 of my Bear Babies weigh _?_ kg.

   A) 3   B) 20   C) 45   D) 75

   8.

9. $24 \div 8 = 48 \div$ _?_

   A) 3   B) 4   C) 6   D) 16

   9.

10. Which does *not* equal $30+30+30$?

    A) $15+60+15$ B) $20+30+40$
    C) $25+30+35$ D) $40+15+40$

    10.

11. How many odd numbers are greater than 10 and less than 20?

    A) 4   B) 5   C) 6   D) 7

    11.

Go on to the next page ⟹ **4**

12. When 246 is divided by 8, the remainder is

    A) 1   B) 2   C) 4   D) 6

12.

13. During his magic act, 1 out of every 3 of Magic Marv's 24 rabbits disappeared. How many rabbits disappeared during Marv's act?

    A) 6   B) 8   C) 12   D) 16

13.

14. $300 + $3 + 300¢ + 3¢ =

    A) $33.33   B) $303.33   C) $306.03   D) $330.60

14.

15. $9 \times 9 \times 9 \times 10 \times 10 \times 10 = 90 \times$ _?_

    A) 3   B) 270   C) 900   D) 8100

15.

16. If I buy 7 apples at 25¢ each, I'll have _?_ left over from my $2.

    A) 25¢   B) 50¢   C) 75¢   D) $1.25

16.

17. $33 + 33 + 33 = 66 + 66 + 66 -$ _?_

    A) 33   B) 66   C) 99   D) 132

17.

18. If it rained on every even-numbered day last April, then on exactly how many days did it rain last April?

    A) 15   B) 16   C) 20   D) 30

18.

19. Which of the following numbers is divisible by both 4 and 8?

    A) 444   B) 484   C) 844   D) 848

19.

20. (20 hundreds) + (20 ones) = _?_ tens

    A) 22   B) 202   C) 220   D) 2020

20.

21. $(1 \times 50) + (5 \times 10) + (10 \times 5) + (50 \times 1) =$

    A) 20   B) 50   C) 200   D) 555

21.

22. If I multiply 2003 by an odd number, then the product *must* be

    A) odd   B) even   C) 2003   D) prime

22.

Go on to the next page ⅢⅢ➡ **4**

11

23. (number of sides a triangle has)×(number of sides a rectangle has) =

    A) 6   B) 7   C) 9   D) 12

23.

24. When I multiply the number
of boys in my youth chorus by
the number of girls, I get 12.
The same is true for Pat's youth
chorus. The number of kids
in Pat's youth chorus *cannot* be

    A) 7   B) 8   C) 9   D) 13

24.

25. Jack is twice as old now as Jill was 4 years ago. If Jack is now
20 years old, then Jill is now ? years old.

    A) 10   B) 14   C) 16   D) 24

25.

26. If the square shown is cut into two pieces
by a straight cut, then the result *cannot* be

    A) 2 triangles   B) 2 same-sized rectangles
    C) 2 squares   D) 2 different-sized rectangles

26.

27. Divide 20 by a whole number that's less than 20. The
remainder *cannot* be

    A) 5   B) 7   C) 9   D) 11

27.

28. One circle's diameter is 8 cm longer than another's. A radius
of the larger circle is ? cm longer than a radius of the smaller.

    A) 2   B) 4   C) 8   D) 16

28.

29. Ali first played tennis 9 days ago.
Since then, Ali has played tennis
every other day. So far, Ali has
played tennis on ? different days.

    A) 4   B) 5   C) 6   D) 9

29.

30. The sum of the 20 smallest positive even whole numbers is 420.
What is the sum of the 20 smallest positive odd whole numbers?

    A) 400   B) 401   C) 419   D) 420

30.

The end of the contest ✍ **4**

Visit our Web site at http://www.mathleague.com

Solutions on Page 77 • Answers on Page 139

2003-2004 Annual 4th Grade Contest

Spring, 2004

Instructions

4

- **Time** You will have only *30 minutes* working time for this contest. You might be *unable* to finish all 30 questions in the time allowed.

- **Scores** Please remember that *this is a contest, not a test*—and there is no "passing" or "failing" score. Few students score as high as 24 points (80% correct). Students with half that, 12 points, *deserve commendation!*

- **Format and Point Value** This is a multiple-choice contest. Each answer is an A, B, C, or D. Write each answer in the *Answer Column* to the right of each question. A correct answer is worth 1 point. Unanswered questions get no credit. You **may** use a calculator.

1. My sixth birthday was three years ago. How old am I now?

   A) 3   B) 6   C) 9   D) 18

2. $20 \times 0 \times 4 =$

   A) $10 \times 2 \times 4$ B) 200×4 C) 20×4 D) $3 \times 0 \times 5$

3. Every woolly mammoth has two tusks. How many tusks do 22 woolly mammoths have in all?

   A) 11   B) 22   C) 44   D) 88

4. 5 quarters = _?_ nickels

   A) 25   B) 50   C) 75   D) 125

5. $1 + 2 + 3 = 11 + 22 + 33 -$ _?_

   A) 30   B) 50   C) 60   D) 66

6. Which is *five hundred fifty-five*, rounded to the nearest ten?

   A) 556   B) 560   C) 565   D) 600

7. If I divide 84 by 84 and then add 84, I get

   A) 84   B) 85   C) 168   D) 252

8. I wrote the same 12-letter message on the blackboard 5 days in a row. How many letters did I write in all?

   A) 12   B) 17   C) 26   D) 60

9. $24 \times 24 = 12 \times 12 \times$ _?_

   A) 2   B) 4   C) 12   D) 144

10. $(9 + 99 + 999) - (9 + 999) =$

    A) 1098   B) 999   C) 108   D) 99

11. 8 dozen = _?_ $\times$ 24 pairs

    A) 2   B) 4   C) 8   D) 12

12. Which of the following sums is an odd number?

    A) 1248 + 8421   B) 8412 + 4812
    C) 8421 + 4821   D) 1248 + 1284

Go on to the next page ⏵ **4**

14

13. The product of 2 whole numbers is 19. What is their sum?

    A) 12   B) 17   C) 20   D) 28

13.

14. What is the tens' digit of the product 2003×2004?

    A) 3   B) 2   C) 1   D) 0

14.

15. If the vowels in my name appear in alpha-
    betical order, then my name could *not* be

    A) Simba   B) Simbo   C) Simbu   D) Simby

15.

16. $36 \div 3 = 3 \times \underline{\ ?\ }$

    A) 33   B) 12   C) 6   D) 4

16.

17. A babysitter earned $6 an hour. By working from 7 P.M. to
    10 P.M. on 7 different days, this babysitter earned

    A) $18   B) $42   C) $72   D) $126

17.

18. $10 \times 1 \times 11 \times 1 \times 10 = 11 \times \underline{\ ?\ }$

    A) 3   B) 10   C) 20   D) 100

18.

19. Exactly how many of the numbers 1, 2, 3, 4, 5, 6, 7, 8, and 9
    are divisible by 3?

    A) 1   B) 2   C) 3   D) 4

19.

20. A taxi carried 6 kids. Each time it stop-
    ped, 1 kid got into the taxi and 2
    kids got out. How many kids were
    in the taxi after it made 3 stops?

    A) 3   B) 6   C) 9   D) 12

20.

21. $4 \times 4 \times 4 =$

    A) 6×6 B) 8×8 C) 12×12 D) 16×16

21.

22. The number of minutes in 1 hour minus the number of hours
    in 1 day is $\underline{\ ?\ }$ the number of seconds in 1 minute.

    A) 36 less than   B) 24 less than   C) 24 more than   D) 36 more than

22.

23. $4 \times$ (diameter of a circle) $= \underline{\ ?\ } \times$ (radius of the same circle)

    A) 2   B) π C) 8   D) 16

23.

Go on to the next page ⟶ **4**

24. Eight years ago, my age plus my dog's age was 18 years. Today the sum of our ages is _?_ years.

    A) 26   B) 34   C) 36   D) 52

    24.

25. Each of the first 99 people on line was given a different number from 1 through 99. How many of those numbers were multiples of 4?

    A) 20   B) 21   C) 24   D) 25

    25.

26. The sum of the lengths of three of the sides of a certain square is 18. What is the perimeter of this square?

    A) 6   B) 24   C) 36   D) 72

    26.

27. Of the following, which number has the largest even divisor?

    A) 888   B) 6666   C) 44 444   D) 222 222

    27.

28. Of 7 tuba players, 4 play in the orchestra and 7 play in the marching band. If every tuba player plays in at least one of the two, how many play in both?

    A) 4   B) 6   C) 7   D) 11

    28.

29. The product of 80 whole numbers is 80. Their sum *cannot* be

    A) 80   B) 88
    C) 90   D) 96

    29.

30. In the diagram, several lines have been drawn through a big triangle whose sides have length 3. Drawing these lines creates some triangles of side-length 1 and some of side-length 2. How many triangles of any of the three sizes appear in the diagram shown?

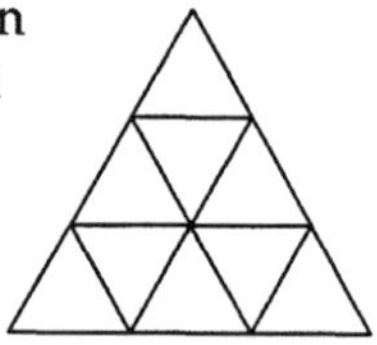

    A) 10   B) 11   C) 12   D) 13

    30.

The end of the contest ✍ **4**

Visit our Web site at http://www.mathleague.com

Solutions on Page 81 • Answers on Page 140

2004-2005 Annual 4th Grade Contest

Spring, 2005

Instructions

4

- **Time** You will have only *30 minutes* working time for this contest. You might be *unable* to finish all 30 questions in the time allowed.

- **Scores** Please remember that *this is a contest, not a test*—and there is no "passing" or "failing" score. Few students score as high as 24 points (80% correct). Students with half that, 12 points, *deserve commendation!*

- **Format and Point Value** This is a multiple-choice contest. Each answer is an A, B, C, or D. Write each answer in the *Answer Column* to the right of each question. A correct answer is worth 1 point. Unanswered questions get no credit. You **may** use a calculator.

1. How many 10¢ gumballs can I buy for $1?

   A) 2   B) 5   C) 10   D) 20

   1.

2. $2 \times 0 \times 0 \times 5 =$

   A) 0   B) 10   C) 100   D) 2005

   2.

3. Ork the stork delivers 2 babies every day. How many babies does Ork deliver in one week?

   A) 2   B) 7   C) 14   D) 21

   3.

4. What number is 5 less than 2 more than 52?

   A) 47   B) 49   C) 54   D) 57

   4.

5. My birthday was Monday. Two days before my birthday was

   A) Saturday   B) Sunday   C) Wednesday   D) Friday

   5.

6. $15-14 + 13-12 + 11-10 + 9-8 + 7-6 + 5-4 =$

   A) 6   B) 7   C) 12   D) 114

   6.

7. What time is it 45 minutes after 4:45?

   A) 4:00   B) 5:00   C) 5:15   D) 5:30

   7.

8. 2 dollars + 20 pennies = 1 dollar + _?_ pennies

   A) 100   B) 120   C) 200   D) 220

   8.

9. Divide 205×205 by 205. The quotient is

   A) 1   B) 2   C) 25   D) 205

   9.

10. A small wheel on my wheelchair has a diameter that's 16 cm long. This small wheel's radius is _?_ cm long.

    A) 4   B) 8   C) 32   D) 196

    10.

11. $1 \times (2 + 3) \times 4 =$

    A) 10   B) 14   C) 20   D) 24

    11.

12. How many 0s are needed to write the numeral for *ten thousand*?

    A) 3   B) 4   C) 5   D) 6

    12.

Go on to the next page ⫸ **4**

13. $60 \times 60 = 20 \times 20 \times \underline{\ ?\ }$ | 13.

   A) 3   B) 9   C) 80   D) 900

14. Three friends and I put dimes in a piggy bank. After the 4 of us put in equal numbers of dimes, I had 3 dimes left over. I put those in the piggy bank too. The total number of dimes we put in the bank *could* have been | 14.

   A) 23   B) 24   C) 25   D) 26

15. $(8-3) \times (2-1) =$ | 15.

   A) 1   B) 3   C) 5   D) 9

16. Each of the following is divisible by 6 *except* | 16.

   A) 3366   B) 4422   C) 6630   D) 6633

17. I'm thinking of a number. When I multiply it by 5, the product is 0. When I multiply the number by 6 instead of by 5, the product is | 17.

   A) 0   B) 1   C) 6   D) 12

18. 10 hundreds + 100 tens = $\underline{\ ?\ }$ ones | 18.

   A) 1000   B) 2000   C) 10 000   D) 20 000

19. The perimeter of my square hammock is 64. How long is each side of my hammock? | 19.

   A) 4   B) 8   C) 16   D) 32

20. If I fold my square hammock exactly in half, the two halves *cannot* be | 20.

   A) triangles   B) rectangles
   C) polygons   D) squares

21. The smallest whole number divisible by both 8 and 12 is | 21.

   A) 4   B) 16   C) 24   D) 48

22. The product of 2005 and any odd number is *always* | 22.

   A) 2005   B) even   C) odd   D) prime

Go on to the next page ⇒ **4**

23. The product of 2 different whole numbers is 7. Their sum is

    A) 6   B) 7   C) 8   D) 14

23.

24. The sum of 2 positive whole numbers is greater than their product if one of the numbers is

    A) 1   B) 2   C) 3   D) 4

24.

25. When I look at our alphabet, I see that the letter _?_ has four times as many letters before it as after it.

    A) E   B) G   C) T   D) U

25.

26. I have 22¢. If I doubled the number of nickels I have, I would then have 37¢. Exactly how many nickels do I have?

    A) 3   B) 4   C) 5   D) 6

26.

27. If paper clips cost 48¢ a dozen, then _?_ paper clips cost $1.

    A) 24   B) 25   C) 26   D) 96

27.

28. Lee, Pat, and Sam bought ice pops. Lee bought 3 times as many as Pat. Sam bought twice as many as Lee. If Sam bought 18 ice pops, how many did Pat buy?

    A) 1   B) 3   C) 6   D) 9

28.

29. Along a straight road, an ice cream vendor is 2 km from the bus and 5 km from the train. The *least* possible distance between the bus and the train is

    A) 3 km   B) 5 km   C) 7 km   D) 10 km

29.

30. My giant sunflower doubles its size every day. On Saturday, it is _?_ times as big as it was on the preceding Sunday.

    A) 2   B) 6   C) 49   D) 64

30.

The end of the contest **4**

2005-2006 Annual 4th Grade Contest

Spring, 2001

Instructions

4

- **Time** You will have only *30 minutes* working time for this contest. You might be *unable* to finish all 30 questions in the time allowed.

- **Scores** Please remember that *this is a contest, not a test*—and there is no "passing" or "failing" score. Few students score as high as 24 points (80% correct). Students with half that, 12 points, *deserve commendation!*

- **Format and Point Value** This is a multiple-choice contest. Each answer is an A, B, C, or D. Write each answer in the *Answer Column* to the right of each question. A correct answer is worth 1 point. Unanswered questions get no credit. You **may** use a calculator.

2005-2006 4TH GRADE CONTEST

1. I had $3 and I spent 3¢. The amount of money I have left is

   A) $2.70   B) $2.93   C) $2.97   D) $3.03

2. $20 \times 0 \times 6 =$

   A) 0   B) 26   C) 120   D) 2006

3. My teacher pointed to a square board with a perimeter of 24. How long is one side of this square?

   A) 4   B) 6   C) 8   D) 20

4. $36 \div 3 = 4 \times \underline{?}$

   A) 12   B) 9   C) 8   D) 3

5. When I round 5555 to the nearest hundred, I get

   A) 5600   B) 5560   C) 5550   D) 5500

6. $10 - 9 + 8 - 7 + 6 - 5 + 4 - 3 + 2 - 1 =$

   A) 10   B) 7   C) 6   D) 5

7. It takes $\underline{?}$ pairs of horseshoes to shoe 14 horses.

   A) 7   B) 14   C) 28   D) 56

8. The product of 8 and 4 equals twice the product of 4 and

   A) 2   B) 4   C) 8   D) 16

9. $(30 + 40 + 50 + 60) - (50 + 60 + 70) =$

   A) 70   B) 40   C) 30   D) 0

10. If grandpa rides my horse for 20 minutes daily, it will take him $\underline{?}$ days to ride my horse a total of 2 hours.

    A) 3   B) 4   C) 6   D) 10

11. 9 hundreds + 9 tens + 99 ones =

    A) 9999   B) 1089   C) 999   D) 989

12. If tomorrow is 3 days before Tuesday, then today is

    A) Friday   B) Saturday   C) Sunday   D) Thursday

Go on to the next page IIII➡ **4**

13. It rained every odd-numbered day in March, a total of _?_ days.

A) 15   B) 16   C) 29   D) 31

13.

14. If $8 in quarters weighs 200 g,
then $3 in quarters weighs

A) 50 g   B) 60 g   C) 75 g   D) 80 g

14.

15. Which *cannot* be rewritten as $1 \times 2 \times 3 \times 4 \times 5$?

A) 12×15 B) 6×20 C) 24×5 D) 30×4

15.

16. $16 + 16 + 16 = 36 + 36 + 36 - \underline{\ ?\ }$

A) 20   B) 30   C) 40   D) 60

16.

17. I have $1 in nickels and $2 in
dimes. That's a total of _?_ coins.

A) 60   B) 40   C) 30   D) 20

17.

18. $64 + 64 + 64 = 8 \times \underline{\ ?\ }$

A) 8   B) 12   C) 16   D) 24

18.

19. The shaded region is bounded by squares of
side-lengths 4 and 8. What is the sum of the in-
ner and outer perimeters of the shaded region?

A) 48   B) 36   C) 32   D) 16

19.

20. $(1 \times 1 \times 1) + (2 \times 2 \times 2) + (3 \times 3 \times 3) + (4 \times 4 \times 4) =$

A) 10×10 B) 12×34 C) $1+4+9+16$ D) $12+34$

20.

21. Of the following, _?_ is divisible
by the *most* whole numbers.

A) 38   B) 48   C) 58   D) 68

21.

22. If Ann was the 9th person in
line and Bob was the 27th person
in line, how many people were
in line between Ann and Bob?

A) 16   B) 17   C) 18   D) 19

22.

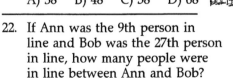

23. If 2 whole numbers differ
by 2, their product *cannot* be

A) 15   B) 35   C) 105   D) 195

23.

Go on to the next page ⫸ **4**

23

24. For each throw, our only possible scores are 0, 3, and 5. Our total score after 4 throws *cannot* be

    A) 7   B) 9
    C) 11   D) 13

24.

25. The average of my age this year and my age 2 years ago is 10. How old will I be 1 year from now?

    A) 10   B) 11   C) 12   D) 13

25.

26. At an amusement park, it costs $172 for tickets for 2 adults and 2 children. If tickets for 2 adults and 1 child cost $134, then 1 adult ticket costs

    A) $38   B) $46   C) $48   D) $68

26.

27. The largest divisor of $1 \times 2 \times 3 \times 4 \times 5$ is

    A) 4   B) 5   C) 20   D) 120

27.

28. If 1 tic = 2 tacs and 3 tacs = 4 toes, then 8 toes = _?_ tics.

    A) 2   B) 3   C) 4   D) 6

28.

29. The larger square has twice the perimeter of the smaller. If the perimeter of the larger is 16, what is the perimeter of the shaded region, as shown?

    A) 8   B) 10   C) 12   D) 16

29.

30. I have 25 coins, all pennies, nickels, dimes, and quarters, whose total value is $3.53. If I doubled the number of dimes, the total value of all the coins would be $4.33. I have exactly _?_ quarters.

    A) 9   B) 10   C) 11   D) 12

30.

The end of the contest ✍ **4**

Visit our Web site at http://www.mathleague.com

Solutions on Page 89 • Answers on Page 142

24

5th Grade Contests

•••••••••••••••••••••••••

2001-2002 through 2005-2006

2001-02 Annual 5th Grade Contest

Spring, 2002

Instructions

5

- **Time** Do *not* open this booklet until you are told by your teacher to begin. You will have only *30 minutes* working time for this contest. You might be *unable* to finish all 30 questions in the time allowed.

- **Scores** Please remember that *this is a contest, not a test*—and there is no "passing" or "failing" score. Few students score as high as 24 points (80% correct). Students with half that, 12 points, *should be commended!*

- **Format and Point Value** This is a multiple-choice contest. Each answer is an A, B, C, or D. Write each answer in the *Answer Column* to the right of each question. A correct answer is worth 1 point. Unanswered questions get no credit. You **may** use a calculator.

1. $30 + 31 + 32 = 29 + 30 + 31 + \underline{\ ?\ }$

   A) 0   B) 1   C) 2   D) 3

   1.

2. $(3 \times 4 \times 5 \times 6) \div 15 =$

   A) 8   B) 10   C) 12   D) 24

   2.

3. Frank is the 5th person in a line of 44 people. How many people are behind Frank and in front of the last person on the line?

   A) 34   B) 38   C) 39   D) 49

   3.

4. $7 + 14 + 21 = 7 \times \underline{\ ?\ }$

   A) 6   B) 5   C) 4   D) 3

   4.

5. 20 hundreds + 2 ones =

   A) 202   B) 222   C) 2002   D) 2020

   5.

6. When each book is shared by 2 students, 40 students will need

   A) 20 books   B) 40 books   C) 60 books   D) 80 books

   6.

7. If I climb 12 trees a day, I'll need $\underline{\ ?\ }$ days to climb 300 trees.

   A) 12   B) 20   C) 25   D) 36

   7.

8. $45 \div 3 = 3 \times \underline{\ ?\ }$

   A) 20   B) 15   C) 10   D) 5

   8.

9. Early Bird ate 36 worms, each either fat or thin. If Early Bird ate 3 times as many fat worms as thin, how many fat worms did Early Bird eat?

   A) 9   B) 24   C) 27   D) 30

   9.

10. Of the following quotients, which is a multiple of 3?

    A) $120 \div 3$ B) $150 \div 3$ C) $180 \div 3$ D) $210 \div 3$

    10.

11. What is the sum of two whole numbers whose product is 48 and whose difference is 8?

    A) 12   B) 16   C) 18   D) 24

    11.

Go on to the next page ⏵ **5**

2001-2002 5TH GRADE CONTEST

12. 1 entire day + 60 hours = 3 entire days + ? hours

   A) 1   B) 12   C) 20   D) 24

13. There were as many kids in the first car of the roller coaster as the largest possible sum of two different one-digit numbers. How many kids is that?

   A) 16   B) 17   C) 18   D) 19

14. $1000 \times 10 \times 0 \times 10 \times 1000 =$

   A) $100\,000 \times 0$ B) 1000×1000 C) 100×1000 D) $10 \times 10\,000$

15. (# of sides of a triangle) $\times$ (# of sides of an octagon) = (# of sides of a square) $\times$ (# of sides of a ?)

   A) triangle   B) rectangle   C) pentagon   D) hexagon

16. What is the average of 1, 9, 11, 19, 21, 29, 31, and 39?

   A) 19   B) 20   C) 21   D) 40

17. The value of my 12 quarters is less than the value of your

   A) 3 dollars   B) 60 nickels   C) 120 dimes   D) 300 pennies

18. The polygon with the fewest number of sides has ? sides.

   A) 1   B) 2   C) 3   D) 4

19. What number is 99 less than the quotient 9999 ÷ 99?

   A) 0   B) 2   C) 200   D) 9999

20. What is the ones' digit of the product $79 \times 79 \times 79$?

   A) 9   B) 7   C) 3   D) 1

21. I eat 18 dozen bowls of honey every 48 minutes. In 8 hours, I eat ? bowls of honey.

   A) 108   B) 180   C) 216   D) 2160

22. The sum of the digits of the greatest multiple of 7 that's less than 1000 is

   A) 7   B) 18   C) 21   D) 22

23. My piggy bank contained only nickels and dimes. If there were 2 more nickels than dimes, then the value of all of these coins could *not* be

    A) 25¢   B) 40¢   C) 55¢   D) 75¢

    23.

24. The 2002nd positive odd whole number is

    A) 4001   B) 4003   C) 4004   D) 4005

    24.

25. How many pairs of parallel sides does a square have?

    A) 4   B) 3   C) 2   D) 1

    25.

26. When our alphabet is written in alphabetical order, which letter has four times as many letters before it as after it?

    A) E   B) F   C) T   D) U

    26.

27. In every magic square, the sum of the numbers in each row, each column, and each major diagonal is called the *magic sum*. What number must I add to each number in the magic square shown at the right to increase its magic sum from 15 to 30?

    | 4 | 9 | 2 |
    | 3 | 5 | 7 |
    | 8 | 1 | 6 |

    A) 5   B) 7   C) 8   D) 15

    27.

28. Pat writes one of the numbers 1, 2, 3, 4, or 5. Lee writes one of the numbers 6, 7, 8, 9, or 10. The two written numbers could have any of _?_ different possible products.

    A) 5   B) 10   C) 21   D) 25

    28.

29. The quotient 189 ÷ _?_ does *not* have a remainder of 3.

    A) 15   B) 31   C) 62   D) 186

    29.

30. Each of the 300 students in my school played miniature golf exactly 2 of the past 5 nights. The average number of these students playing each night was

    A) 100   B) 120   C) 150   D) 600

    30.

The end of the contest ✍ **5**

2002-03 Annual 5th Grade Contest

Spring, 2003

Instructions

5

- **Time** Do *not* open this booklet until you are told by your teacher to begin. You will have only *30 minutes* working time for this contest. You might be *unable* to finish all 30 questions in the time allowed.

- **Scores** Please remember that *this is a contest, not a test*—and there is no "passing" or "failing" score. Few students score as high as 24 points (80% correct). Students with half that, 12 points, *should be commended!*

- **Format and Point Value** This is a multiple-choice contest. Each answer is an A, B, C, or D. Write each answer in the *Answer Column* to the right of each question. A correct answer is worth 1 point. Unanswered questions get no credit. You **may** use a calculator.

1. The sum 4+5+6 is _?_ less than the sum 14+15+16. A) 7 B) 10 C) 20 D) 30	1.
2. The value of 1 quarter + 2 dimes + 3 nickels + 4 pennies is A) 41¢ B) 64¢ C) 75¢ D) $1.41	2.
3. My sea serpent, 39 m long, painted colored rings, each 3 m wide, around its body. That's at most _?_ rings. A) 3 B) 9 C) 13 D) 117	3.
4. $(2 \times 4 \times 6 \times 8) \div 32 =$ A) 6 B) 8 C) 10 D) 12	4.
5. Dumbo eats 3 bags of peanuts every hour. In 24 hours, he eats A) 8 bags B) 21 bags C) 27 bags D) 72 bags	5.
6. The quotient $42 \div 2$ has the same value as the product A) 3×6 B) 3×7 C) 3×14 D) 3×21	6.
7. I own 16 leashes, 2 for for each dog I own. I own _?_ dogs. A) 8 B) 16 C) 17 D) 32	7.
8. 8 hundreds − 8 tens = A) 820 B) 792 C) 720 D) 700	8.
9. Which of the following figures has a positive *even* number of sides? A) hexagon B) circle C) pentagon D) triangle	9.
10. How many buses that hold 50 students each are needed to carry 150 4th graders, 200 5th graders, and 250 6th graders to a circus? A) 3 B) 7 C) 9 D) 12	10.
11. $(2 \times 4) + (3 \times 4) + (4 \times 4) + (5 \times 4) = 4 \times$ _?_ A) 8 B) 14 C) 20 D) 120	11.
12. I last rode my motorized mini-bike on June 1. I first rode it 60 days before, on A) March 31 B) April 1 C) April 2 D) April 3	12.
13. Of the following quotients, which is greater than 3? A) $162 \div 54$ B) $174 \div 87$ C) $186 \div 63$ D) $136 \div 45$	13.

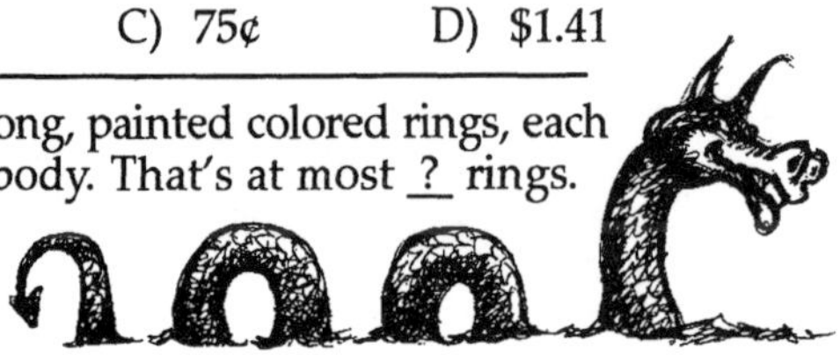

Go on to the next page ⫸ **5**

14. Which number is 1 less than the 10 thousands' digit of 987 654?

    A) 4   B) 5   C) 7   D) 8

15. 14.

15. The total value of my 5 heart sculptures is $2. Their average value is

    A) 4¢   B) 10¢
    C) $10   D) 40¢

15.

16. $3 \times 20 \times 100 = 30 \times \underline{\ ?\ }$

    A) 2×100 B) 2×10 C) 20×100 D) 200×100

16.

17. If a circle's diameter is 6 m long, then its radius is _?_ long.

    A) 3 m   B) 6 m   C) 12 m   D) 18 m

17.

18. I get the same result when I multiply or divide 80 by

    A) 0   B) 1   C) 2   D) 80

18.

19. What is the time 8 hours and 8 minutes *before* 7:07 P.M.?

    A) 3:15 A.M.   B) 5:15 A.M.   C) 9:59 A.M.   D) 10:59 A.M.

19.

20. My class of 30 kids has 6 more boys than girls. It has _?_ boys.

    A) 12   B) 18   C) 20   D) 24

20.

21. Multiply 111 by 444. The product has _?_ odd digit(s).

    A) zero   B) one   C) three   D) nine

21.

22. A board has alternating dark and light squares, just like a checker-board, except that there are 9 squares on each side, instead of 8. At most how many of the squares on this 9×9 board are dark?

    A) 38   B) 39   C) 40   D) 41

22.

23. Ted turned 10 years old yesterday. If I average his ages, in years, on his 5 most recent birthdays, I'll get

    A) 6   B) 7   C) 8   D) 9

23.

Go on to the next page ⫸ **5**

33

24. Multiply the first 100 positive whole numbers. The ones' digit is

A) 2   B) 4   C) 8   D) 0

24.

25. Each of the 66 gloves my mom owns is is either black or blue. If twice as many of her gloves are black as are blue, how many *pairs* of *blue gloves* does she own?

A) 11   B) 22   C) 44   D) 132

25.

26. In a pile of 60 coins, half are nickels and one-third are dimes. The value of the nickels is _?_ than the value of the dimes.

A) 50¢ less   B) 50¢ more   C) 10¢ less   D) 10¢ more

26.

27. Al's plant had 10 flowers when he got it. For every flower that wilted, 2 new ones bloomed. If 8 flowers have wilted since Al got his plant, how many flowers now bloom on Al's plant?

A) 16   B) 18   C) 20   D) 26

27.

28. Using the rule "Do not lift your pencil or fold the paper," it's NOT possible to draw a path connecting points *X* and *Y* without crossing the curve. Using the same rule, it IS possible to connect points *X* and

A) *A*   B) *B*   C) *C*   D) *D*

28.

29. I burp at a steady rate of 3 times every 10 minutes. You burp at a steady rate of 4 times every 12 minutes. Together, we burp _?_ times every _?_ minutes.

A) 7, 22   B) 11, 15
C) 13, 20   D) 19, 30

29.

30. A rectangular room is 20 m wide and 30 m long. On the room's floor, along its outer edge, I painted a white strip 2 m wide. What is the area of the strip?

A) 96 m^2 B) 100 m^2 C) 184 m^2 D) 200 m^2

30.

The end of the contest **5**

Visit our Web site at http://www.mathleague.com

Solutions on Page 99 • Answers on Page 144

34

2003-2004 Annual 5th Grade Contest

Spring, 2004

Instructions

5

- **Time** Do *not* open this booklet until you are told by your teacher to begin. You will have only *30 minutes* working time for this contest. You might be *unable* to finish all 30 questions in the time allowed.

- **Scores** Please remember that *this is a contest, not a test*—and there is no "passing" or "failing" score. Few students score as high as 24 points (80% correct). Students with half that, 12 points, *should be commended!*

- **Format and Point Value** This is a multiple-choice contest. Each answer is an A, B, C, or D. Write each answer in the *Answer Column* to the right of each question. A correct answer is worth 1 point. Unanswered questions get no credit. You **may** use a calculator.

1. What day is 3 days before Thursday?

   A) Monday   B) Tuesday   C) Saturday   D) Sunday

   1.

2. $2 + 12 + 22 = 1 + 11 + 21 + \underline{?}$

   A) 1   B) 2   C) 3   D) 4

   2.

3. My school lunch costs me 10 nickels and 10 dimes. This lunch costs me

   A) \$1.10   B) \$1.20   C) \$1.50   D) \$2

   3.

4. $(45 \div 5) + (36 \div 4) + (27 \div 3) = 9 \times \underline{?}$

   A) 1   B) 3   C) 6   D) 12

   4.

5. The product of 27 and 3 equals the product of $\underline{?}$ and 27.

   A) 3   B) 9   C) 81   D) 243

   5.

6. $6 + 12 + 18 + 24 + 30 = 6 \times \underline{?}$

   A) 10   B) 12   C) 13   D) 15

   6.

7. 10×10 has the same value as

   A) $100 \div 10$ B) $1000 \div 10$ C) $100 \div 100$ D) $1000 \div 100$

   7.

8. $110 \times 10 \times 0 \times 10 \times 110 =$

   A) 0   B) 100   C) 240   D) 12 100

   8.

9. Together, my scooter's two wheels cost \$22. The rear wheel costs \$4 more than the front wheel. The front wheel costs

   A) 18   B) 13   C) 11   D) 9

   9.

10. A roller coaster ride costs 3 tickets. A ferris wheel ride costs 2 tickets. To go on both rides 5 times, I need $\underline{?}$ tickets.

    A) 5   B) 10   C) 25   D) 30

    10.

11. The sum of 54 320 and 54 321 has $\underline{?}$ digits.

    A) 5   B) 6   C) 10   D) 11

    11.

Go on to the next page ⟶ **5**

36

12. $7 + 7 - 7 + 7 - 7 + 7 =$ A) 0 B) 7 C) 14 D) 21	12.
13. If I travel 30 km each hour, I will travel _?_ in 300 minutes. A) 10 km B) 15 km C) 100 km D) 150 km	13.
14. Juan was 10 years old 10 years ago. In 20 years, his age will be A) 10 B) 20 C) 30 D) 40	14.
15. I caught a big fish. It weighed 120 kg, which is 3 times as much as I weigh. I weigh _?_ kg. A) 30 B) 40 C) 60 D) 360	15.
16. $3 \times 3 \times 3 \times 3 \times 3 \times 3 =$ A) 9×9 B) $9 + 9$ C) $9 \times 9 \times 9$ D) $9 + 9 + 9$	16.
17. If the only positive factors of a number greater than 1 are itself and 1, then the number must be A) prime B) odd C) even D) composite	17.
18. Of the following numbers, which is the largest? A) 9 ones B) 7 tens C) 5 hundreds D) 3 thousands	18.
19. (perimeter of a square) ÷ (length of one side of the square) = A) 1 B) 2 C) 4 D) 16	19.
20. Twice Baby Bird's current age in hours equals three times Baby Bird's age one hour ago. Baby Bird is _?_ hours old. A) 2 B) 3 C) 4 D) 6	20.
21. Which expression is *not* divisible by 9? A) $9 - 9$ B) $9 + 9$ C) 9×9 D) $9 \div 9$	21.
22. In the sequence 11, 13, 15, . . . , 95, 97, 99, there are 45 odd numbers. How many of them have an even tens' digit? A) 20 B) 22 C) 23 D) 25	22.

Go on to the next page ▐▐▶ **5**

23. Multiply my favorite whole number by 8, then round to the nearest 10. You'll get 130. The sum of the digits of my favorite number is

    A) 6   B) 7   C) 8   D) 9

    23.

24. By playing on the Music Truck, more than 4 friends (but fewer than 9) earned a total of $88.92. If each got the same pay, how much was each paid?

    A) $17.78   B) $14.82
    C) $12.70   D) $11.12

    24.

25. The value of my money in *whole* dollars is the same as the total value of 250 identical coins. These coins could be

    A) dimes   B) nickels   C) pennies   D) quarters

    25.

26. If each of the numbers 2, 4, 8, 16 is increased by 2, then the sum of the 4 numbers will increase by

    A) 2   B) 4   C) 8   D) 16

    26.

27. We'll call two letters *cousins* if the same number of line segments are needed to form each. For example, the letters **W** and **E** are cousins, but **K** and **L** are not. The letter **L** is a cousin of the letter

    A) **C**   B) **F**   C) **H**   D) **V**

    27.

28. Ballet Bear can do 72 pirouettes (twirls) in 12 minutes. At the same rate, how many pirouettes can Ballet Bear do in 3 minutes?

    A) 6   B) 12   C) 18   D) 24

    28.

29. What is the smallest positive integer that is divisible by 1, 2, 3, 4, and 5?

    A) 720   B) 360   C) 120   D) 60

    29.

30. The perimeter of a field is a prime number. The length of each side is a whole number. The field could *not* be in the shape of a

    A) triangle   B) hexagon   C) pentagon   D) rectangle

    30.

The end of the contest **5**

2004-2005 Annual 5th Grade Contest

Spring, 2005

Instructions

5

- **Time** Do *not* open this booklet until you are told by your teacher to begin. You will have only *30 minutes* working time for this contest. You might be *unable* to finish all 30 questions in the time allowed.

- **Scores** Please remember that *this is a contest, not a test*—and there is no "passing" or "failing" score. Few students score as high as 24 points (80% correct). Students with half that, 12 points, *should be commended!*

- **Format and Point Value** This is a multiple-choice contest. Each answer is an A, B, C, or D. Write each answer in the *Answer Column* to the right of each question. A correct answer is worth 1 point. Unanswered questions get no credit. You **may** use a calculator.

1. $200 + 300 + 400 = 100 + 200 + 300 + \underline{?}$

   A) 100   B) 200   C) 300   D) 400

   1.

2. To fill a big hole, I used 2 fewer than 2-dozen truckloads of dirt. I used $\underline{?}$ truckloads of dirt.

   A) 10   B) 12   C) 20   D) 22

   2.

3. $27 \div 3 = 3 \times \underline{?}$

   A) 3   B) 6   C) 9   D) 27

   3.

4. I threw 9 coins into the air. If twice as many coins landed heads up as landed tails up, how many coins landed heads up?

   A) 3   B) 4   C) 5   D) 6

   4.

5. If you subtract 19 ones from 19 tens, the result is

   A) 1871   B) 342   C) 171   D) 9

   5.

6. $4 \times 8 \times 12 = 16 \times \underline{?}$

   A) 32   B) 24   C) 20   D) 16

   6.

   What's up?

7. If my neck grows 5 cm every 10 days, it takes $\underline{?}$ days for my neck to grow 50 cm.

   A) 5   B) 10   C) 25   D) 100

   7.

8. $(33 + 44 + 55 + 66) \div 11 =$

   A) 18   B) 11   C) 9   D) 7

   8.

9. Of the following, which is divisible by 6?

   A) 166   B) 266   C) 366   D) 466

   9.

10. Pete paid for 4 identical frozen pizzas with a $20 bill. If Pete got $3.60 in change, how much did one frozen pizza cost?

    A) $4.10   B) $5   C) $6.25   D) $9

    10.

11. $(48 \times 2) + (48 \times 3) + (48 \times 4) = 48 \times \underline{?}$

    A) 24   B) 9   C) 5   D) 3

    11.

Go on to the next page ⟹ **5**

12. (perimeter of my square) ÷ (sum of 2 side-lengths of my square) =

A) 1   B) 2   C) 4   D) 8

12.

13. Tom is 12 years old. What is the average of his age 4 years ago and his age 6 years ago?

A) 11   B) 7   C) 5   D) 4

13.

14. I was wandering around the house at 12 hours and 12 minutes before noon. I was wandering around at

A) 11:48 A.M.   B) 12:12 A.M.
C) 11:48 P.M.   D) 12:12 P.M.

14.

15. Two million equals

A) 200×100 B) 200×1000 C) 2000×1000 D) $20\,000 \times 10$

15.

16. The number 2005 is a 4-digit number. What is the sum of the *greatest* 3-digit number and the *greatest* 4-digit number?

A) 9998   B) 9999   C) 10 000   D) 10 998

16.

17. If an ape ate 1 banana every 4 hours, it ate ? bananas in 5 days.

A) 20   B) 24   C) 30   D) 120

17.

18. One side of an equilateral triangle is 6 cm long. The triangle's perimeter is ? cm.

A) 2   B) 6   C) 18   D) 36

18.

19. The school meeting is on the 199th day of the calendar year, in

A) May B) June C) July D) August

19.

20. The number 728 is divisible by all of the following *except*

A) 7   B) 8   C) 28   D) 72

20.

21. I multiplied 1111×1111 and wrote down the product. When I wrote the product, the largest *odd* digit that I wrote was

A) 1   B) 3   C) 4   D) 5

21.

Go on to the next page ⏵ **5**

41

22. The product of my number and twice my number is 72. What is half my number?

    A) 3   B) 6   C) 12   D) 36

    Incredible!

22.

23. Mary got either a 90 or a 100 on each of her 5 math tests. The average of all her math tests is 98. How many 90s did she get?

    A) 1   B) 2   C) 3   D) 4

23.

24. In the division (121 121 121 006)÷(11), the remainder is

    A) 6   B) 5   C) 4   D) 3

24.

25. The greatest common divisor of 60, 160, and 260 is

    A) 5   B) 6   C) 20   D) 60

25.

26. The sum of 5 consecutive whole numbers is 2005. What is the sum of all the digits of these 5 numbers?

    A) 15   B) 25   C) 34   D) 43

26.

27. If 3 splishes = 2 splashes, then 18 splashes = ? splishes.

    A) 12   B) 27   C) 36   D) 48

27.

28. Of the 100 numbers 1, 2, 3, . . . , 100, how many are both 5 more than some number in the list *and* 5 less than some other number in the list?

    A) 89   B) 90   C) 91   D) 100

28.

29. How many 2-digit whole numbers are multiples of *both* 6 and 9?

    A) 2   B) 3   C) 4   D) 5

29.

30. If 2+4+6+. . .+100 = 2550, then 1+3+5+. . .+99 =

    A) 2400   B) 2450   C) 2500   D) 2550

30.

The end of the contest ✍ **5**

2005-2006 Annual 5th Grade Contest

Spring, 2006

Instructions

5

- **Time** Do *not* open this booklet until you are told by your teacher to begin. You will have only *30 minutes* working time for this contest. You might be *unable* to finish all 30 questions in the time allowed.

- **Scores** Please remember that *this is a contest, not a test*—and there is no "passing" or "failing" score. Few students score as high as 24 points (80% correct). Students with half that, 12 points, *should be commended!*

- **Format and Point Value** This is a multiple-choice contest. Each answer is an A, B, C, or D. Write each answer in the *Answer Column* to the right of each question. A correct answer is worth 1 point. Unanswered questions get no credit. You **may** use a calculator.

1. $9 + 9 + 9 + 9 + 9 = 18 + 18 + \underline{\ ?\ }$

   A) 0   B) 9   C) 18   D) 36

   1.

2. A snail that crawls 50 m each hour crawls 225 m in $\underline{\ ?\ }$ hours.

   A) 4   B) $4\frac{1}{2}$ C) 5   D) $5\frac{1}{2}$

   2.

3. There are $\underline{\ ?\ }$ socks in 12 pairs of socks.

   A) 6   B) 12   C) 24   D) 48

   3.

4. The total weight of 7 giant carrots, each weighing 700 g, is $\underline{\ ?\ }$ g.

   A) 100   B) 490   C) 700   D) 4900

   4.

5. $(11 + 10 + 1) - (11 - 10 - 1) =$

   A) 22   B) 11   C) 10   D) 0

   5.

6. In value, 10 nickels + 10 dimes = 15 $\underline{\ ?\ }$.

   A) pennies   B) nickels
   C) dimes   D) quarters

   6.

7. By how much does the sum of the digits in List K exceed the sum of the digits in List L?

   List K: 3 1 6 9 5 2 8 7

   List L: 2 0 5 8 4 1 7 6

   A) 1   B) 8   C) 33   D) 41

   7.

8. Which of the following has a value greater than 3?

   A) $30 \div 11$ B) $31 \div 12$ C) $35 \div 12$ D) $43 \div 14$

   8.

9. 4 P.M. is $\underline{\ ?\ }$ minutes after 3:40 P.M.

   A) 20   B) 30   C) 40   D) 60

   9.

10. If all beavers work at the same rate, and if 6 beavers can clear the trees from a lot in 36 hours, how many hours would it take 12 beavers to clear these same trees?

    A) 18   B) 24   C) 54   D) 72

    10.

11. The perimeter of a square is 24. The total length of 3 of its sides is

    A) 6   B) 8   C) 12   D) 18

    11.

Go on to the next page ⮕ **5**

12. If 20 is subtracted from 4 times _?_ , the result is 100. A) 20 B) 30 C) 80 D) 120	12.
13. In the large "magic" square shown, the sums of the numbers in every row and column are equal. What number should appear in the empty cell? A) 41 B) 49 C) 50 D) 51	13.

34	153	68
119	85	
102	17	136

14. The sum of 2 different odd numbers greater than 0 could be A) 2 B) 3 C) 4 D) 5	14.
15. My 11 books have a total of 2175 pages. If 5 of my books have 315 pages each, then my other 6 books have a total of _?_ pages. A) 700 B) 600 C) 550 D) 500	15.
16. 6002 is 2006 more than A) 3996 B) 4004 C) 4006 D) 8008	16.
17. This year, the lovebirds had 16 sets of triplets. There are as many birds in 16 sets of triplets as there are in _?_ sets of twins. A) 4 B) 8 C) 12 D) 24	17.
18. Twice the number of pencils I have equals 3 times the number you have. If I have 24 pencils, then you have _?_ pencils. A) 4 B) 8 C) 12 D) 16	18.
19. How many days before tomorrow is 2 days before yesterday? A) 5 B) 4 C) 3 D) 2	19.
20. The number of non-zero digits in the product of 3000 and 30 000 is A) 1 B) 2 C) 3 D) 9	20.
21. An octagon has _?_ times as many sides as a trapezoid. A) 1 B) 2 C) 3 D) 4	21.
22. How many even numbers are greater than 2 and less than 100? A) 48 B) 49 C) 50 D) 98	22.

Go on to the next page ‖➡ **5**

23. I paid $1 for 4 pens. You paid 40¢ for 2. You saved _?_ on each. A) 5¢　　　B) 15¢　　　C) 20¢　　　D) 25¢	23.
24. If my age now plus my age 6 years ago is 24, in 2 years I'll be A) 11　　B) 15　　C) 17　　D) 20	24.
25. Today, I delivered 3 pink boxes and 2 blue boxes. Each pink box weighed the same. Each blue box weighed the same. The total weight of the 3 pink boxes equaled the total weight of the 2 blue boxes. The 5 boxes weighed 60 kg altogether. How much did each blue box weigh? A) 12 kg　B) 15 kg　C) 20 kg　D) 30 kg	25.
26. Divide $6 \times 7 \times 8 \times 9 \times 10$ by $1 \times 2 \times 3 \times 4 \times 5$. The remainder is A) 63　　B) 9　　C) 7　　D) 0	26.
27. If I fold the piece of cardboard shown so each little square is a different side of a cube, what number will be on the side opposite the side numbered 6? A) 5　　　B) 3　　　C) 2　　　D) 1	27.

28. Dad took $205 from his $300 bank account to buy me a toy. The bank deducts $5 every month Dad has less than $100 in that account. How many months will it take for Dad's bank account to become $0?
  A) 17　　　　B) 18
  C) 19　　　　D) 20
	28.

29. If $1+2+3+ \ldots +100 = 5050$, then $101+102+103+ \ldots +200 =$ A) 10 000　　B) 10 050　　C) 10 100　　D) 15 050	29.
30. There are exactly _?_ different ways that I can rearrange the digits of 1234 to form a number greater than 1234. A) 3　　　B) 11　　　C) 17　　　D) 23	30.

The end of the contest ✍ **5**

6th Grade Contests

2001-2002 through 2005-2006

2001-2002 Annual 6th Grade Contest

Tuesday, March 12 or 19, 2002

Instructions

6

- **Time** You will have only *30 minutes* working time for this contest. You might be *unable* to finish all 40 questions in the time allowed.

- **Scores** Please remember that *this is a contest, not a test*—and there is no "passing" or "failing" score. Few students score as high as 30 points (75% correct). Students with half that, 15 points, *should be commended!*

- **Format and Point Value** This is a multiple-choice contest. Each answer is an A, B, C, or D. Write each answer in the *Answers* column to the right of each question. A correct answer is worth 1 point. Unanswered questions get no credit. You **may** use a calculator.

1. What is the difference between 34 343 and 1212? A) 13 133 B) 22 223 C) 32 222 D) 33 131		1.
2. $(100 - 40) + (90 - 30) + (80 - 20) = 3 \times \underline{\ ?\ }$ A) 20 B) 60 C) 80 D) 180		2.
3. When $(9999 + 999 + 99 + 4)$ is divided by 9, the remainder is A) 1 B) 3 C) 4 D) 5		3.
4. Divide one million by five hundred thousand. The quotient is A) 2 B) 10 C) 20 D) 50		4.
5. $2^4 - 2^3 - 2^2 - 2^1 = 16 - \underline{\ ?\ }$ A) 1 B) 2 C) 14 D) 15		5.
6. Jo is the 12th of 25 people to get her pen "biggie-sized" at McBurgers. How many people are there *between* Jo and the 25th person on line? A) 11 B) 12 C) 13 D) 14		6.
7. What is the sum of the first four odd whole numbers? A) 6 B) 9 C) 10 D) 16		7.
8. What is the tens' digit of the product $22\,222 \times 22\,222$? A) 8 B) 6 C) 4 D) 2		8.
9. $8777 - 7778 = 444 + \underline{\ ?\ }$ A) 445 B) 455 C) 545 D) 555		9.
10. Altogether, if 12 of our small elephant balloons weigh 130 kg, then 72 of these same balloons weigh A) 190 kg B) 650 kg C) 780 kg D) 864 kg		10.
11. 500 is midway between 350 and A) 200 B) 650 C) 700 D) 850		11.
12. The number of dimes in \$4 equals the number of quarters in A) \$6 B) \$8 C) \$10 D) \$40		12.
13. How many different positive factors are common to 36 and 48? A) 4 B) 5 C) 6 D) 8		13.
14. The smallest composite number *without* 2, 3, or 5 as a factor is A) 41 B) 49 C) 67 D) 77		14.
15. The average of sixteen 4s, times the average of four 16s, equals A) 4×16 B) 16×16 C) 16×64 D) 64×64		15.

16. The number 2002 is the product of exactly __?__ positive primes. | 16.
    A) 2   B) 3   C) 4   D) 5

17. Counting 3 million birds at a rate | 17.
    of 80 birds per minute takes
    A) 470 minutes   B) 625 minutes
    C) 2500 minutes D) 37 500 minutes

18. $(10^3 \times 1000) + (10^2 \times 100) + (10^1 \times 10) =$ | 18.
    A) $10^6 + 10^4 + 10^2$ B) $2 \times (10^3 + 10^2 + 10^1)$
    C) 10^{12} D) $10^9 + 10^4 + 10^1$

19. Of the following, which has the greatest value? | 19.
    A) 20% of 80   B) 25% of 65   C) 30% of 50   D) 35% of 35

20. How many different whole numbers are factors of 120? | 20.
    A) 5   B) 11   C) 15   D) 16

21. If the product of 3 whole numbers is even, their sum must be | 21.
    A) even   B) odd   C) prime   D) whole

22. What is the sum of 5 numbers whose average is 5 more than 5? | 22.
    A) 10   B) 25   C) 50   D) 125

23. For the first 50 whole numbers, the ratio (primes):(even numbers) is | 23.
    A) 15:25 B) 16:25   C) 15:35   D) 16:34

24. $\sqrt{(25-9) + (25-9) + (25-9) + (25-9)} =$ | 24.
    A) $\sqrt{4 \times 16}$ B) $4 \times \sqrt{16}$
    C) $6 + \sqrt{100}$ D) $\sqrt{100} - \sqrt{36}$

25. After Sam spent 35% of his money on a gift, | 25.
    he had $13 left. How much did the gift cost?
    A) $6   B) $7   C) $20   D) $23

26. The largest whole number which satisfies __?__ :7 < 7:16 is | 26.
    A) 2   B) 3   C) 4   D) 5

27. The 5th of 9 consecutive whole numbers whose sum is 153 is | 27.
    A) 9   B) 13   C) 17   D) 21

28. The sum of any 3 angles of a rectangle is | 28.
    A) 120°   B) 180°   C) 270°   D) 360°

29. Jack was 8 when Jill was 2. Now | 29.
    that Jack is twice as old as Jill, he
    is teaching her how to ice skate.
    The sum of their ages now is
    A) 8   B) 9   C) 12   D) 18

30. The product of 4 different whole numbers could *not* equal | 30.
    A) 2^4 B) 2^6 C) 2^8 D) 2^{12}

31. Each of 5 bikers sang a duet with each of | 31.
    the others. A total of ? duets were sung.
    A) 10   B) 15   C) 20   D) 25

32. $200^3 \div 100^3 = 200 \div$? | 32.
    A) 100   B) 80   C) 25   D) 8

33. How many whole numbers less than 1000 are *not* divisible by 4? | 33.
    A) 875   B) 850   C) 800   D) 750

34. If the sum of 2 whole numbers is 76, their product is at most | 34.
    A) 5776   B) 5700   C) 1444   D) 1443

35. Between 1901 and 2001, it was possible for a period of 5 con- | 35.
    secutive calendar years to contain a total of ? days.
    A) 1825   B) 1827   C) 1828   D) 1830

36. A plane left New York at 2 P.M. | 36.
    and landed in Vancouver 6 hours
    later. If New York time is 3 hours
    ahead of Vancouver time, when did
    the plane land, in Vancouver time?
    A) 11 P.M.   B) 9 P.M.   C) 8 P.M.   D) 5 P.M.

37. If a radius of one circle with area 16π cm^2 is used as a diameter | 37.
    of a second circle, how far apart are the centers of the two circles?
    A) 2 cm   B) 4 cm   C) 6 cm   D) 8 cm

38. If $51 + 52 + \ldots + 100 = 3775$, then $101 + 102 + \ldots + 150 =$ | 38.
    A) 8775   B) 7550   C) 6275   D) 3825

39. The sum of 1999 positive whole numbers is 2002. What is the least | 39.
    possible number of 1s that can be used as addends in this sum?
    A) 1995   B) 1996   C) 1997   D) 1998

40. What is the name of the only regular polygon which has as | 40.
    many diagonals as it has sides?
    A) square   B) pentagon   C) hexagon   D) octagon

The end of the contest **6**

2002-2003 Annual 6th Grade Contest

Tuesday, March 11 or 18, 2003

6

Instructions

- **Time** You will have only *30 minutes* working time for this contest. You might be *unable* to finish all 40 questions in the time allowed.

- **Scores** Please remember that *this is a contest, not a test*—and there is no "passing" or "failing" score. Few students score as high as 30 points (75% correct). Students with half that, 15 points, *should be commended!*

- **Format and Point Value** This is a multiple-choice contest. Each answer is an A, B, C, or D. Write each answer in the *Answers* column to the right of each question. A correct answer is worth 1 point. Unanswered questions get no credit. You **may** use a calculator.

1.	$20+60 = 20 \times \underline{?}$ A) 2 B) 3 C) 4 D) 6	1.
2.	Today, Tim's age + Kim's age = 28. Two years ago, this sum was A) 24 B) 26 C) 30 D) 32	2.
3.	I eat 50 drops of melting ice cream each minute. How many minutes will it take for me to eat 150 drops of ice cream? A) $1\frac{1}{2}$ B) 2 C) $2\frac{1}{2}$ D) 3	3.
4.	$(9+1+8+2) \div (7+3+6+4) =$ A) 0 B) 1 C) 5 D) 20	4.
5.	(# sides of square) $-$ (# sides of triangle) = A) 7 B) 4 C) 3 D) 1	5.
6.	$144 \times 60 = 72 \times \underline{?}$ A) 72 B) 120 C) 132 D) 140	6.
7.	8 and 4 have the same greatest common factor as 8 and A) 12 B) 14 C) 16 D) 40	7.
8.	The expressions 9×89 and $\underline{?}$ have the same value. A) 9×98 B) 899×1 C) $899 - 98$ D) $989 - 89$	8.
9.	The ratio (# of digits in one million) : (# of digits in ten thousand) = A) 2:1 B) 6:5 C) 7:5 D) 5:3	9.
10.	$6400 \div 80 = 80 \times \underline{?}$ A) 1 B) 80 C) 800 D) 6400	10.
11.	In our alphabet, 24 times as many letters come before $\underline{?}$ as after. A) X B) B C) C D) Y	11.
12.	Mr. Sheep, there's no need to worry! *Sheepskin* is just slang for the college diploma you got 3 days before the day after Tuesday, which was a A) Wed. B) Fri. C) Sat. D) Sun.	12.
13.	If every carton holds 12 eggs, then 60 cartons hold $\underline{?}$ eggs. A) 12 dozen B) 60 dozen C) 144 dozen D) 720 dozen	13.
14.	$789+98 = 89+ \underline{?}$ A) 987 B) 878 C) 798 D) 177	14.
15.	The smallest possible product of two different prime numbers is A) 0 B) 3 C) 5 D) 6	15.
16.	$3^2 + 4^2 =$ A) 5^2 B) 7^2 C) 12^2 D) 34^2	16.

Go on to the next page ⫸ **6**

17. If the sum of two numbers equals their difference, their product is A) 0 B) 1 C) 2 D) 4	17.
18. _?_ is the product of two whole numbers whose difference is 1. A) 63 B) 80 C) 90 D) 99	18.
19. On vacation, my front teeth hurt on 4 days. That was half as many days as they were OK. My vacation lasted _?_ days. A) 2 B) 6 C) 8 D) 12	19.
20. The average of 4 km and 400 cm is _?_ m. A) 202 B) 220 C) 2002 D) 22 000	20.
21. Each of 12 pizzas was cut into 8 slices, and *everyone* ate 2 slices. If exactly 4 slices remained uneaten, then _?_ people ate pizza. A) 46 B) 48 C) 92 D) 96	21.
22. If a rectangle with area 36 is *not* a square, its width *cannot* be A) 4 B) 6 C) 9 D) 12	22.
23. How many whole numbers are factors of both 28 and 32? A) 2 B) 3 C) 4 D) 5	23.
24. The least common multiple of 4 and 6 is A) 2 B) 6 C) 12 D) 24	24.
25. I had _?_ polka dots on my clown costume, and that's 1 more than a prime number! A) 46 B) 48 C) 50 D) 53	25.
26. Al has $1.50. Di has $2.25. Gumballs cost 15¢ each, so Di can buy _?_ more than Al. A) 5 B) 10 C) 15 D) 25	26.
27. Round the sum 3.83 + 2.34 to the nearest tenth. A) 6.1 B) 6.17 C) 6.18 D) 6.2	27.
28. If 31 minutes ago was noon, then 31 minutes from now is A) 12:31 A.M. B) 1:02 A.M. C) 12:31 P.M. D) 1:02 P.M.	28.
29. If the larger of two consecutive whole numbers has one more digit than the smaller, then the sum of their ones' digits is A) 10 B) 9 C) 1 D) 0	29.

Go on to the next page ⟫ **6**

30. Dave ran 2 km at 8 km per hr. Andy ran 2 km at 10 km per hr. It took Dave _?_ more minutes than Andy to run the 2 km. A) 2 B) 3 C) 12 D) 15	30.
31. If you add my age 10 years ago to my age 10 years from now, then the sum will be _?_ times my current age. A) 2 B) 3 C) 4 D) 10	31.
32. If a dinosaur takes 2003 seasons to become an adult, then one born in the winter would become an adult in the A) spring B) summer C) autumn D) winter	32.
33. If 2 gulps = 5 slurps, and 2 slurps = 7 sips, then 35 sips = A) 3 gulps B) 4 gulps C) 5 gulps D) 7 gulps	33.
34. If a rectangle whose width is half its length has an area of 18, then a square of the same width has an area of A) 6 B) 9 C) 27 D) 36	34.
35. My address is a two-digit number. The product and the sum of these two digits are equal. This two-digit number is A) 10 B) 11 C) 21 D) 22	35.
36. If I read 1 book every 2 weeks, it takes me _?_ to read 52 books. A) 26 weeks B) 52 weeks C) 54 weeks D) 104 weeks	36.
37. Every whole number *not* divisible by 2, 3, 4, 5, 6, 7, 8, or 9 *must* be A) even B) prime C) odd D) negative	37.
38. Exactly how many hours does it take for a minute hand to go 60 times completely around the face of a circular clock? A) 1 B) 60 C) 360 D) 3600	38.
39. There are _?_ 3-digit whole numbers between 99 and 1000. A) 1000 B) 999 C) 900 D) 899	39.
40. If the sum of the areas of three squares is 29, and if their sides are consecutive integers, then a side of the largest square is A) 4 B) 5 C) 9 D) 16	40.

The end of the contest **6**

Visit our Web site at http://www.mathleague.com

Solutions on Page 121 • Answers on Page 149

2003-2004 Annual 6th Grade Contest

Tuesday, March 9 or 16, 2004

Instructions

6

- **Time** You will have only *30 minutes* working time for this contest. You might be *unable* to finish all 40 questions in the time allowed.

- **Scores** Please remember that *this is a contest, not a test*—and there is no "passing" or "failing" score. Few students score as high as 30 points (75% correct). Students with half that, 15 points, *should be commended!*

- **Format and Point Value** This is a multiple-choice contest. Each answer is an A, B, C, or D. Write each answer in the *Answers* column to the right of each question. A correct answer is worth 1 point. Unanswered questions get no credit. You **may** use a calculator.

1. When an odd number is divided by 2, the remainder is always

     A) 0   B) 1   C) 2   D) prime

       1.

2. Of 60 men wearing a ball and chain, twice as many prefer stripes as prefer solids. How many prefer stripes?

     A) 15   B) 20   C) 30   D) 40

       2.

3. ? is the square of a whole number.

     A) 4444   B) 444   C) 44   D) 4

       3.

4. $88 \times 44 = 11 \times 11 \times$?

     A) 12   B) 20   C) 32   D) 122

       4.

5. Twice my age, plus 9, is 37. How old am I?

     A) 14   B) 15   C) 19   D) 28

       5.

6. $(110+120+130+140)-(10+20+30+40) =$

     A) 270   B) 310   C) 330   D) 400

       6.

7. $2^2+2^2+2^2+2^2 =$ A) 4^2 B) 8^2 C) 16^2 D) 22^2

       7.

8. The expression $7 \times 7 + 7 \times 7$ has the same value as ? $\times 7$.

     A) 14   B) 21   C) 49   D) 56

       8.

9. (number of digits in 1 000 000) : (number of digits in 12 million) =

     A) 1:12   B) 1:2   C) 3:4   D) 7:8

       9.

10. $111+999 = 5 \times$?   A) 110   B) 111   C) 220   D) 222

       10.

11. What is the difference between the area and the perimeter of a square with side-length 6?   Writer's block?

     A) 6   B) 12   C) 18   D) 24

       11.

12. At my fastest, I can carve 40 letters a day. At that rate, I'll need ? days to carve 180 letters.

     A) 4   B) $4\frac{1}{2}$ C) 5   D) $5\frac{1}{2}$

       12.

13. 11 hundreds = 111 tens − ?

     A) 0   B) 1   C) 10   D) 11

       13.

14. 25% of one hour = ? minutes

     A) 10   B) 12   C) 15   D) 25

       14.

15. $3^2 \times 3^2 \div 3 = 3 \times$?   A) 1   B) 3   C) 3^2 D) 3^3

       15.

16. (989 rounded to the nearest ten) − (989) =

     A) 0   B) 1   C) 3   D) 10

       16.

Go on to the next page ⫸ **6**

17. Each *face* of a cube is a square. A cube has _?_ faces.
    A) 2　　　　　B) 3　　　　　C) 4　　　　　D) 6

17.

18. What is the largest odd divisor of 2004?
    A) 3　　　　　B) 167　　　　　C) 501　　　　　D) 1001

18.

19. The average degree-measure of the angles of a triangle is
    A) 30°　　　　B) 45°　　　　C) 60°　　　　D) 90°

19.

20. Half my number is 6. My number's square is
    A) 9　　B) 36　　C) 81　　D) 144

20.

21. A triangle with whole number sides has perimeter 6. How many of these sides must have the same length?
    A) 3　　　　　B) 2
    C) 1　　　　　D) 0

21.

22. The value of 3×4 quarters equals the value of 5×6 _?_ .
    A) dimes　　B) dollars　　C) nickels　　D) pennies

22.

23. Each of the following has four divisors *except*
    A) 6　　　　　B) 8　　　　　C) 9　　　　　D) 10

23.

24. $\sqrt{4^2 + 4^2 + 4^2 + 4^2} = 2 \times$ _?_
    A) 4　　　　　B) 8　　　　　C) 4^2　　　　D) 8^2

24.

25. Exactly how many prime numbers less than 40 have 2 digits?
    A) 7　　　　　B) 8　　　　　C) 13　　　　　D) 14

25.

26. Of 30 hands, 10 point left, 10 point right, and 10 don't point at all. I need to have _?_ of these 30 hands to be certain that I have at least 2 left-pointing hands.
    A) 6　　B) 11　　C) 21　　D) 22

26.

27. The largest of 5 consecutive whole numbers whose average is 10 is
    A) 10　　B) 12　　C) 13　　D) 15

27.

28. I have equal numbers of quarters, dimes, nickels, and pennies. The value of these coins could be any of the following *except*
    A) 41¢　　　B) $1.23　　C) $1.68　　D) $2.46

28.

29. If 30% of a number is 60, then 70% of the number is
    A) 70　　　　B) 100　　　　C) 130　　　　D) 140

29.

30. I was half my current age 10 years ago, so 4 years ago my age was
    A) 20　　　　B) 16　　　　C) 14　　　　D) 6

30.

Go on to the next page ⫸ **6**

31. Four identical squares, lined up as shown, form a rectangle whose area is 144. What is the perimeter of the shaded region?

    A) 36   B) 48   C) 60   D) 108

    31.

32. If the product of 6 different positive integers is 120 000, then what is the greatest possible value of one of the 6 integers?

    A) 1000   B) 2000   C) 3000   D) 6000

    32.

33. If every gumball weighs 3 g, then a machine holding 3 kg of gumballs holds ? gumballs.

    A) 100   B) 300   C) 1000   D) 3000

    33.

34. How many 3-digit numbers greater than 100 read the same forwards and backwards, like 575?

    A) 81   B) 90   C) 99   D) 100

    34.

35. If the first of 1000 consecutive whole numbers is odd, their sum must be

    A) even   B) odd   C) prime   D) negative

    35.

36. You'll get a triangle if you connect any 3 of the dots at the right. You can get at most ? different such triangles.

    A) 2   B) 3   C) 4   D) 5

    36.

37. Any of the ten digits 0 through 9 may be used in a 6-digit code, but no digit may be used more than once. If the first two digits are 1 and 7, what is the largest possible *average* of all 6 digits?

    A) 4   B) 6   C) $6\frac{1}{2}$ D) 7

    37.

38. Coach ran 4 km in 30 minutes. He ran the first 2 km at a constant speed that was twice the constant speed at which he ran the last 2 km. Coach ran the third km at a speed of ? km/hr.

    A) 4   B) 6   C) 8   D) 12

    38.

39. Of the following products, which has the most prime factors?

    A) 1×121 B) 11×15
    C) 7×19 D) 6×35

    39.

40. A month with 30 days had 5 Saturdays and 5 Sundays. The first day of that month had to fall on a

    A) Thursday   B) Friday   C) Saturday   D) Sunday

    40.

The end of the contest ✍ **6**

Visit our Web site at http://www.mathleague.com

Solutions on Page 125 • Answers on Page 150

2004-2005 Annual 6th Grade Contest

Tuesday, March 8, 2005

6

Instructions

- **Time** You will have only *30 minutes* working time for this contest. You might be *unable* to finish all 40 questions in the time allowed.

- **Scores** Please remember that *this is a contest, not a test*—and there is no "passing" or "failing" score. Few students score as high as 30 points (75% correct). Students with half that, 15 points, *should be commended!*

- **Format and Point Value** This is a multiple-choice contest. Each answer is an A, B, C, or D. Write each answer in the *Answers* column to the right of each question. A correct answer is worth 1 point. Unanswered questions get no credit. You **may** use a calculator.

1. Of the following, which is between $\frac{1}{2}$ and $\frac{3}{4}$? A) 0.2 B) 0.4 C) 0.6 D) 0.8	1.
2. A polygon *cannot* have _?_ sides. A) 2 B) 3 C) 4 D) 21	2.
3. The brochure said, "Watch your mail!" I watched for 5 days less than 5 weeks. For how many days did I watch my mail? A) 10 B) 25 C) 30 D) 35	3.
4. $1010 + 10\,100 = 10 \times$ _?_ A) 101 B) 1010 C) 1020 D) 1111	4.
5. A \$5 roll of dimes has _?_ more coins than a \$10 roll of quarters. A) 0 B) 2 C) 5 D) 10	5.
6. If 10% of a number is 100, then 100% of the same number is A) 10 B) 100 C) 110 D) 1000	6.
7. $(12+10+8+6+4+2) \div (6+5+4+3+2+1) =$ A) 60 B) 45 C) 6 D) 2	7.
8. Which of the following numbers is *twice* a multiple of 6? A) 28 B) 30 C) 36 D) 42	8.
9. $54 \div 3 = 3 \times$ _?_ A) 6 B) 18 C) 54 D) 162	9.
10. A roll of wallpaper covers half the area of a square wall whose width is 4. The area of the part covered by this wallpaper is A) 4 B) 8 C) 16 D) 32	10.
11. I need 12 pieces of fruit to make 3 glasses of juice. How many pieces of fruit do I need to make 10 glasses of juice? A) 30 B) 36 C) 40 D) 120	11.
12. How many positive divisors of 100 are also multiples of 100? A) 1 B) 10 C) 25 D) 100	12.
13. A *hendecagon* is an 11-sided polygon. What is the product of the number of sides of a hendecagon and of a square? A) 44 B) 55 C) 66 D) 88	13.
14. (number of 0s in 1 thousand):(number of 0s in 1 million) = A) 1:1 B) 1:2 C) 2:3 D) 4:7	14.
15. Every _?_ number has at least one even prime factor. A) even B) odd C) prime D) whole	15.

Go on to the next page ▐▐▐➡ **6**

16. If my pet runs 300 *cm*/sec. and your rocket flies 300 *m*/sec., then your rocket travels _?_ times as fast as my pet. A) 30 000 B) 10 000 C) 300 D) 100	16.
17. I multiply 2 integers. Their product is 32. Their sum *cannot* be A) 12 B) 18 C) 32 D) 33	17.
18. The average of 11, 12, 13, 14, 15, 16, 17, 18, and 19 is A) 15 B) 16 C) 19 D) 135	18.
19. In a 3-act play, each act has 4 scenes. If 2 new characters are introduced in each scene, how many characters are in this play? A) 6 B) 8 C) 12 D) 24	19.
20. If $\frac{3}{4}$ of our letters are bills, then the ratio of the number of bills to the number of other letters is **We Get Letters..** A) 7:1 B) 7:3 C) 3:1 D) 3:4	20.
21. $4 \times 4^4 =$ A) 4^4 B) 4^5 C) 14^4 D) 16^5	21.
22. Ten coins, each a penny, a nickel, or a dime, *cannot* total A) 11¢ B) 19¢ C) 30¢ D) 31¢	22.
23. The area of a square with integer side-lengths *could* be A) 600 B) 700 C) 800 D) 900	23.
24. The total value of 75 nickels = the total value of _?_ quarters. A) 3 B) 15 C) 25 D) 375	24.
25. The following are all factors of $30 \times 40 \times 50$ *except* A) $1 \times 3 \times 5$ B) $2 \times 4 \times 6$ C) $5 \times 7 \times 9$ D) $6 \times 8 \times 10$	25.
26. Ten years ago, the sum of the ages of Ted and his twin brother Todd was 22. How old is Ted now? A) 16 B) 21 C) 32 D) 42	26.
27. We have 6 tents for 18 campers. Each tent holds either 2 or 4 campers. Exactly how many of our tents hold 2? A) 4 B) 3 C) 2 D) 1	27.
28. If 3 out of 5 dentists recommend sugarless gum, what percent *don't* recommend sugarless gum? A) 20% B) 30% C) 40% D) 60%	28.
29. The time _?_ is 6 hours before 6 minutes after noon. A) 6:06 A.M. B) 6:06 P.M. C) 5:54 A.M. D) 5:54 P.M.	29.

Go on to the next page ⮕ 6
63

30. The *digit-sum* of a whole number is the sum of its digits. How many whole numbers between 9 and 100 have an even digit-sum? A) 45 B) 48 C) 50 D) 52	30.
31. At a rate of 80 km/hr., I can run _?_ km in 18 minutes. A) 20 B) 24 C) 28 D) 30	31.
32. $2^{2005} = 2^{2004} + \underline{?}$ A) 1 B) 2 C) 2004 D) 2^{2004}	32.
33. The sum of the digits of all positive primes less than 20 is A) 77 B) 76 C) 41 D) 40	33.
34. If 2 pears weigh as much as 3 peaches, and 2 peaches weigh as much as 30 grapes, then _?_ pears weigh as much as 90 grapes. A) 4 B) 6 C) 8 D) 12	34.
35. A square with a perimeter of 32 is split into 8 identical triangles, as shown. What is the sum of the areas of the 4 shaded triangles? A) 4 B) 8 C) 16 D) 32	35.
36. The sum of the 50 whole numbers 51, 52, . . . , 100 is _?_ greater than the sum of the 50 whole numbers 1, 2, . . . , 50. A) 2000 B) 2500 C) 2550 D) 5000	36.
37. Service without a smile costs twice as much as service with a smile. I spent $360 for 110 services, 100 with a smile, and 10 without a smile. Each service with a smile cost me A) $3.00 B) $3.15 C) $3.30 D) $3.45	37.
38. What is the *total* number of times that the hour hand, minute hand, and second hand go around a circular clock in 1 day? A) 144 B) 1440 C) 1466 D) 86 400	38.
39. The product of 3 different primes is always divisible by exactly _?_ different non-prime numbers greater than 1. A) 1 B) 2 C) 3 D) 4	39.
40. Every birthday of my life, I put as many pennies in a jar as my age in years. I now have $1.20 in the jar. How old am I? A) 10 B) 12 C) 15 D) 20	40.

The end of the contest ✍ **6**

Visit our Web site at http://www.mathleague.com

Solutions on Page 129 • Answers on Page 151

2005-2006 Annual 6th Grade Contest

Tuesday, February 28, 2006

Instructions

6

- **Time** You will have only *30 minutes* working time for this contest. You might be *unable* to finish all 40 questions in the time allowed.

- **Scores** Please remember that *this is a contest, not a test*—and there is no "passing" or "failing" score. Few students score as high as 30 points (75% correct). Students with half that, 15 points, *should be commended!*

- **Format and Point Value** This is a multiple-choice contest. Each answer is an A, B, C, or D. Write each answer in the *Answers* column to the right of each question. A correct answer is worth 1 point. Unanswered questions get no credit. You **may** use a calculator.

1. $75+25+76+24 =$
   A) 200   B) 201   C) 202   D) 203

   1.

2. If 3 pies require 2 dozen apples, then 6 pies require _?_ apples.
   A) 12   B) 18   C) 36   D) 48

   2.

3. If I add 8 nines or 18 _?_, I get the same sum.
   A) threes B) fours C) nines D) nineteens

   3.

4. If 2 of every 3 dancing bears wear red tutus, then _?_ of 24 dancing bears wear red tutus.
   A) 8   B) 12   C) 16   D) 18

   4.

5. $20 \times 30 \times 40 = 60 \times$ _?_
   A) 300 B) 400 C) 500 D) 1200

   5.

6. What is the tens' digit of 55×55?
   A) 7   B) 5   C) 3   D) 2

   6.

7. The sum of the measures of all the angles in a triangle is
   A) 360°   B) 270°   C) 180°   D) 90°

   7.

8. The month that's 3 months after Mar. is _?_ months before Oct.
   A) 1   B) 2   C) 3   D) 4

   8.

9. Divide 305 by 25 and find the remainder. Now divide 3005 by that remainder. What is the remainder in this second division?
   A) 0   B) 5   C) 95   D) 160

   9.

10. $2 \div 1 = (22+44) \div$ _?_
    A) $(2+4)$ B) 11   C) 22   D) $(11+22)$

    10.

11. Divide the area of a circle by the area of its semi-circle.
    A) 4   B) 1/4   C) 1/2   D) 2

    11.

12. How many prime numbers are even?
    A) 0   B) 1   C) 2   D) 3

    12.

13. Our town's mayor gives speeches all the time. So far this year, he's made $2+2^2+5+5^2$ speeches. How many is that?
    A) $7+7^2$ B) 6^2 C) 10^2 D) 14^2

    13.

14. $1800 \div 30$ has the same value as $30 \times$ _?_.
    A) 2   B) 6   C) 54   D) 60

    14.

15. If a rectangle has integer sides, its perimeter must be
    A) even   B) odd   C) 4   D) prime

    15.

Go on to the next page ⫸ **6**

16. Written as a numeral, *eight hundred thousand fifty* has _?_ 0s. A) 3 B) 4 C) 5 D) 6	16.
17. It takes me _?_ days to mail 600 000 cards if I mail 3000 each day. A) 100 B) 200 C) 1000 D) 2000	17.
18. If the perimeter of a pentagon is 60, its average side-length is A) 6 B) 10 C) 12 D) 15	18.
19. Giant sandwiches come prepackaged. I can buy 1 for $30, 3 for $75, or 5 for $100. If I have $425 to spend, and I buy at least one of these packages, then I can buy *at most* _?_ giant sandwiches. A) 18 B) 19 C) 20 D) 21	19.
20. Of the 10 factors of 48, how many are divisible by 2? A) 5 B) 7 C) 8 D) 9	20.
21. The ones' digit of the product of the first 33 primes is A) 0 B) 2 C) 4 D) 6	21.
22. All sides of a _?_ can have different lengths. A) rhombus B) rectangle C) square D) triangle	22.
23. The greatest common factor of $2 \times 3 \times 4 \times 5$ and $6 \times 7 \times 8 \times 9$ is A) 6 B) 8 C) 24 D) 48	23.
24. Each year, my allowance doubles from the previous year. My allowance is now $2. Three years ago, my allowance was A) 25¢ B) 50¢ C) 70¢ D) 75¢	24.
25. What time is it 1111 minutes after 11:11 A.M.? A) 5:11 A.M. B) 5:40 A.M. C) 5:42 A.M. D) 6:01 A.M.	25.
26. My team alternately won and lost all of our 101 games. If we won 13 of our first 25 games, then we won _?_ of our last 15 games. A) 7 B) 8 C) 12 D) 13	26.
27. 75% of a 12-slice pizza is _?_ slices. A) 7 B) 8 C) 9 D) 10	27.
28. $3^2 + 4^2 + 12^2 =$ A) 13^2 B) 15^2 C) 17^2 D) 19^2	28.
29. If the sum (my age in years) + (my age in months) is 65, then in 5 years, I'll be _?_ years old. A) 9 B) 10 C) 11 D) 12	29.

Go on to the next page ⫸ **6**

30. If a cartoon lasts at least 5 minutes and at most 8 minutes, then 3 cartoons could *not* last a total of _?_ minutes. A) 15 B) 18 C) 24 D) 25	30.
31. At what time each day does the hour hand complete its first revolution around the face of a circular clock? A) 1 A.M. B) 1 P.M. C) midnight D) noon	31.
32. The total weight of 1 blue and 4 red sacks is 40 kg. If the average weight of all 5 sacks is twice the weight of the blue sack, the average weight of 1 red sack is _?_ kg. A) 36 B) 9 C) 8 D) 4	32.
33. Square S has area 36. The biggest circle that fits inside S has area A) 3π B) 6π C) 9π D) 36π	33.
34. The greatest common factor of 2 different primes is always A) odd B) even C) prime D) 0	34.
35. If 1 hip = 3 hops, and if 2 hops = 5 hip-hops, then _?_ hips = 15 hip-hops. A) 2 B) 3 C) 5 D) 6	35.
36. I sell 3 tickets every 10 minutes. You sell 4 tickets every 12 minutes. If we sell at these rates and work together, then we sell a total of _?_ tickets every _?_ minutes. A) 7, 9 B) 11, 15 C) 12, 20 D) 19, 30	36.
37. If I multiply a whole number by _?_ and then add 1 to the product, the result is *never* divisible by 5. A) 2 B) 3 C) 4 D) 5	37.
38. A square of area 144 is divided into 4 identical smaller squares, as shown. Each smaller square is divided into 2 triangles. The area of the shaded region is A) 72 B) 36 C) 18 D) 12	38.
39. If the sum of 10 consecutive whole numbers is 5005, then the sum of the next 10 consecutive whole numbers is A) 5015 B) 5050 C) 5105 D) 50 105	39.
40. 180 million seconds is the same length of time as _?_ hours. A) 5 000 000 B) 50 000 C) 5000 D) 50	40.

The end of the contest ☝ **6**

Visit our Web site at http://www.mathleague.com

Solutions on Page 133 • Answers on Page 152

Detailed Solutions

• • • • • • • • • • • • • • • •

2001-2002 through 2005-2006

4th Grade Solutions

2001-2002 through 2005-2006

Information & Solutions

Spring, 2002

Contest Information

4

- **Solutions** Turn the page for detailed contest solutions (written in the question boxes) and letter answers (written in the *Answer Column* to the right of each question).

- **Scores** Please remember that *this is a contest, not a test*—and there is no "passing" or "failing" score. Few students score as high as 24 points (80% correct). Students with half that, 12 points, *deserve commendation!*

- **Answers & Rating Scale** Turn to page 138 for the letter answers to each question and the rating scale for this contest.

1. The product of any number and 0 is 0, so $20 \times 0 \times 2 = 0$.
    A) 0 B) 40 C) 400 D) 2002

    1.

    A

2. 5 more than $7 = 12$, so 3 more than "5 more than 7" $= 3+12 = 15$.
    A) 8 B) 10 C) 12 D) 15

    2.

    D

3. We toasted 8 dozen marshmallows at our campfire. That's $8 \times 12 = 96$ marshmallows.
    A) 12 B) 20 C) 64 D) 96

    3.

    D

4. $(9-8) + (7-6) + (5-4) + (3-2) = 4 = 1 + 3.$
    A) 3 B) 4 C) 5 D) 8

    4.

    A

5. If I had 9¢ more, I'd have $1, so I now have $100¢ - 9¢ = 91¢$.
    A) 90¢ B) 91¢ C) 99¢ D) $1.09

    5.

    B

6. If a plant blooms for exacty 3 months each year, that same plant does *not* bloom for exactly $12-3 = 9$ months each year.
    A) 3 B) 6 C) 9 D) 12

    6.

    C

7. $1+1+10+10+100+100 = (1+10+100) + (1+10+100) = 111+111.$
    A) 89 B) 99 C) 111 D) 121

    7.

    C

8. The following birds were standing under a pear tree: 4 calling birds, 3 French hens, 2 turtle doves, and 1 partridge. That's a total of $4+3+2+1 = 10$ birds standing under the pear tree.
    A) 9 B) 10 C) 11 D) 24

    8.

    B

9. Since 7 days after Tuesday is a Tuesday, 6 days after Tuesday is a Monday.
    A) Sat. B) Sun. C) Mon. D) Wed.

    9.

    C

10. The sum of four 5s $= 5+5+5+5 = 20 = 4 \times 5$.
    A) $4 + 5$ B) 4×5 C) 45 D) 5555

    10.

    B

11. $12 \times 12 = 3 \times 2 \times 2 \times 12 = 3 \times 48 = 4 \times 36 = 6 \times 24 = 144$.
    A) 3×48 B) 4×36 C) 6×24 D) 8×16

    11.

    D

Go on to the next page ⠿➡ **4**

12. The seasons are summer, autumn, winter, spring, summer, ... A) winter B) spring C) autumn D) summer	12. D
13. In 12 years, Ali will be twice as old as she is now. She's 12 now; 4 years ago she was 8. A) 8 B) 16 C) 20 D) 28	13. A
14. $22+22+22 = 66 = 33+33+33 - 33.$ A) 11 B) 22 C) 33 D) 66	14. C
15. 10 to 99 is as many #s as $(10-9)$ to $(99-9)$, or 1 to 90, so 90 #s. A) 88 B) 89 C) 90 D) 91	15. C
16. One coin was equal in value to the sum of the other three, so the coins were 1 quarter, 2 dimes, and 1 nickel. Value = 50¢. A) 20¢ B) 25¢ C) 40¢ D) 50¢	16. D
17. When $(12+24+36 + 1)$ is divided by 12, the remainder is 1. A) 0 B) 1 C) 5 D) 9	17. B
18. Of the 18 fish in my aquarium, twice as many have stripes as do not have stripes, so there are 12 with stripes and 6 without. A) 6 B) 9 C) 12 D) 15	18. C
19. If _?_ $\div 99 = 11$, then _?_ $= 11 \times 99 = 1089.$ A) 9 B) 88 C) 999 D) 1089	19. D
20. Every whole number, whether odd or even, is divisible by 1. A) 0 B) 1 C) 2 D) 3	20. B
21. 11 hrs. after 11:11 P.M. is 10:11 A.M.; 11 mins. later is 10:22 A.M. A) 10:22 A.M. B) 12 P.M. C) 12 A.M. D) 12:22 A.M.	21. A
22. Between the first vowel, *a*, and the last consonant, *z*, you'll write the other 24 letters of the alphabet. A) 23 B) 24 C) 25 D) 26	22. B

Go on to the next page ⫸ **4**

23. The number 246 858 642 is *not* divisible by 4 (since 42 is not). A) 2 B) 4 C) 6 D) 9	23. B
24. Since $124 = 1 \times 124 = 2 \times 62 = 4 \times 31$, the smallest possible difference between the two factors is $31 - 4 = 27$. A) 27 B) 31 C) 60 D) 123	24. A
25. Since $\$12 \times 5 = \$60$, $\$30 \times 2 = \$60$, and $50¢ \times 120 = \$60$, either B, C, or D could be the cost of a car wash. Notice that $60 is *not* divisible by $9. A) \$9 B) \$12 C) \$30 D) 50¢	25. A
26. Each circle has a diameter of 4, so I can fit three rows of circles, with 3 circles in each row, inside this square. That's 9 circles. A) 6 B) 9 C) 12 D) 36	26. B
27. A delivery truck carries 8 cases. Each case contains 7 cartons. In each carton are 6 boxes. Since each box contains 1 pie, there are $8 \times 7 \times 6 = 336$ pies. A) 21 B) 62 C) 104 D) 336	27. D
28. $(2-1)+(4-1)+(6-1)+ \ldots +(48-1)+(50-1) = 650-25 = 625$. A) 599 B) 600 C) 625 D) 650	28. C
29. The greatest possible perimeter of this rectangle occurs when the 12 squares are lined up single file to form a 2×24 rectangle. Its perimeter is $2 + 24 + 2 + 24 = 52$. A) 28 B) 32 C) 52 D) 72	29. C
30. The minute hand goes around the clock face once each hr. It takes 12 hrs. for the hr. hand to go once around the clock face. In that time, the min. hand goes around 12 times. A) 12 B) 24 C) 60 D) 720	30. A

The end of the contest 🖎 **4**

Visit our Web site at http://www.mathleague.com

76

Information & Solutions

Spring, 2003

Contest Information

4

- **Solutions** Turn the page for detailed contest solutions (written in the question boxes) and letter answers (written in the *Answer Column* to the right of each question).

- **Scores** Please remember that *this is a contest, not a test*—and there is no "passing" or "failing" score. Few students score as high as 24 points (80% correct). Students with half that, 12 points, *deserve commendation!*

- **Answers & Rating Scale** Turn to page 139 for the letter answers to each question and the rating scale for this contest.

77

Answers

1. When you multiply by 0, the product is 0, so $2 \times 0 \times 0 \times 3 = 0$.

   A) 0 B) 5 C) 6 D) 600

   1. A

2. First, 8 more than 9 = 17. Then, 17 = 10 more than 7.

   A) 7 B) 8 C) 11 D) 19

   2. A

3. $(80-70)+(60-50)+(40-30)+(20-10) = 10+10+10+10 = 40$.

   A) 10 B) 20 C) 30 D) 40

   3. D

4. Since 4 can be written as 2×2, we see that 4 is not prime.

   A) 2 B) 3 C) 4 D) 5

   4. C

5. Since 1 Giantfish weighs 3 times as much as 1 Minifish, 2 of my Giantfish weigh $2 \times 3 = 6$ times as much as my Minifish. My Minifish would eat 6 times its own weight.

   A) 2 B) 3 C) 5 D) 6

   5. D

6. 5 quarters = $5 \times 25¢ = 125¢ = 100¢ + 25¢$ = 10 dimes + 5 nickels.

   A) 5 B) 10 C) 15 D) 20

   6. A

7. (# of hours in a day) ÷ (# of months in a year) = $24 \div 12 = 2$.

   A) 2 B) 6 C) 12 D) 36

   7. A

8. If each Bear Baby weighs 15 kg, then 5 Bear Babies weigh (5×15) kg = 75 kg.

   A) 3 B) 20 C) 45 D) 75

   8. D

9. $24 \div 8 = 3$, and $48 \div 16 = 3$.

   A) 3 B) 4 C) 6 D) 16

   9. D

10. $30+30+30 = 90$, but $40+15+40 = 95$.

    A) $15+60+15 = 90$ B) $20+30+40 = 90$
    C) $25+30+35 = 90$ D) $40+15+40 = 95$

    10. D

11. The 5 odd numbers between 10 and 20 are 11, 13, 15, 17, and 19.

    A) 4 B) 5 C) 6 D) 7

    11. B

Go on to the next page ⟹ **4**

12. $8 \times 30 = 240$, so $246 \div 8 = 30$ with remainder 6.

   A) 1   B) 2   C) 4   D) 6

   12. D

13. During his act, 1 out of every 3 of Magic Marv's 24 rabbits disapeared. Since $24 \div 3 = 8$, it follows that 8 rabbits disappeared during the act.

   A) 6   B) 8   C) 12   D) 16

   13. B

14. $\$300 + \$3 + 300\cancel{c} + 3\cancel{c} = \$303 + \$3.03 = \$306.03$.

   A) $33.33   B) $303.33   C) $306.03   D) $330.60

   14. C

15. $9 \times 9 \times 9 \times 10 \times 10 \times 10 = (9 \times 10) \times (9 \times 9 \times 10 \times 10) = (90) \times (8100)$.

   A) 3   B) 270   C) 900   D) 8100

   15. D

16. Since $7 \times 25\cancel{c} = \$1.75$, I'll have $\$2.00 - \$1.75 = 25\cancel{c}$ left over.

   A) 25¢   B) 50¢   C) 75¢   D) $1.25

   16. A

17. $33 + 33 + 33 = 99$; $66 + 66 + 66 = 198$. Subtract.

   A) 33   B) 66   C) 99   D) 132

   17. C

18. The even-numbered days in April are the 2nd, 4th, 6th, . . . , 28th, and 30th. Rain fell on 15 days last April.

   A) 15   B) 16   C) 20   D) 30

   18. A

19. Every choice listed is divisible by 4, but only 848 is divisible by 8.

   A) 444   B) 484   C) 844   D) 848

   19. D

20. $(20 \times 100) + (20 \times 1) = 2020 = 202 \times 10$.

   A) 22   B) 202   C) 220   D) 2020

   20. B

21. $(1 \times 50) + (5 \times 10) + (10 \times 5) + (50 \times 1) = 50 + 50 + 50 + 50 = 200$.

   A) 20   B) 50   C) 200   D) 555

   21. C

22. 2003 is odd, and the product of any two odd numbers is odd.

   A) odd   B) even   C) 2003   D) prime

   22. A

Go on to the next page ⮕ **4**

23. (# sides a triangle has)×(# of sides a rectangle has) = 3×4 = 12. A) 6 B) 7 C) 9 D) 12	23. D
24. Since 12 = 3×4 = 2×6 = 1×12, the number of kids in Pat's youth chorus could be 3+4 = 7, 2+6 = 8, or 1+12 = 13. The number of kids in Pat's youth chorus *cannot* be 9. A) 7 B) 8 C) 9 D) 13	24. C
25. Jack is twice as old as Jill was 4 years ago. Jack is now 20, so it was 4 years ago that Jill was 10. Today, Jill is 10+4 = 14. A) 10 B) 14 C) 16 D) 24	25. B
26. A) B) D) A) 2 triangles B) 2 same-sized rectangles C) 2 squares D) 2 different-sized rectangles	26. C
27. Divide 20 by 15, 13, and 11 to get respective remainders of 5, 7, and 9. The remainder cannot be 10 or any larger number. A) 5 B) 7 C) 9 D) 11	27. D
28. A radius is half as long as a diameter. One circle's diameter is 8 cm longer than another's. Its radius is (8 cm)÷2 = 4 cm longer. A) 2 B) 4 C) 8 D) 16	28. B
29. Ali first played tennis 9 days ago. Ali also played tennis 7 days ago, 5 days ago, 3 days ago, and 1 day ago. She played tennis on 5 different days. A) 4 B) 5 C) 6 D) 9	29. B
30. Each odd number is 1 less than the corresponding even number. The sum of the 20 smallest positive odd numbers is 420 − 20. A) 400 B) 401 C) 419 D) 420	30. A

The end of the contest ✍ **4**

Visit our Web site at http://www.mathleague.com

Information & Solutions

Spring, 2004

Contest Information

4

- **Solutions** Turn the page for detailed contest solutions (written in the question boxes) and letter answers (written in the *Answer Column* to the right of each question).

- **Scores** Please remember that *this is a contest, not a test*—and there is no "passing" or "failing" score. Few students score as high as 24 points (80% correct). Students with half that, 12 points, *deserve commendation!*

- **Answers & Rating Scale** Turn to page 140 for the letter answers to each question and the rating scale for this contest.

Answers

1. Three years ago, I was 6, so now I'm 6 + 3 = 9 years old.

   A) 3   B) 6   C) 9   D) 18

   1. C

2. Product = 0, so the correct choice is D since it has 0 as a factor.

   A) $10 \times 2 \times 4$ B) 200×4 C) 20×4 D) $3 \times 0 \times 5$

   2. D

3. Every woolly mammoth has two tusks, so 22 woolly mammoths have $22 \times 2 = 44$ tusks.

   A) 11   B) 22   C) 44   D) 88

   3. C

4. $5 \times 25¢ = 25 \times 5¢$.

   A) 25   B) 50   C) 75   D) 125

   4. A

5. $1+2+3 = (11-10)+(22-20)+(33-30) = 11+22+33-(10+20+30)$.

   A) 30   B) 50   C) 60   D) 66

   5. C

6. 550 < *five hundred fifty-five* < 560; this is midway, so round up.

   A) 556   B) 560   C) 565   D) 600

   6. B

7. $(84 \div 84) + 84 = 1 + 84 = 85$.

   A) 84   B) 85   C) 168   D) 252

   7. B

8. I wrote the same 12-letter message on the blackboard 5 days in a row. In all, I wrote $12 \times 5 = 60$ letters.

   A) 12   B) 17   C) 26   D) 60

   8. D

9. $24 \times 24 = 12 \times 2 \times 12 \times 2 = 12 \times 12 \times 4$.

   A) 2   B) 4   C) 12   D) 144

   9. B

10. $(9+99+999) - (9+999) = (9-9) + 99 + (999-999) = 99$.

    A) 1098   B) 999   C) 108   D) 99

    10. D

11. 8 dozen = $8 \times 12 = 96 = 48 \times 2 = 48$ pairs = 2×24 pairs.

    A) 2   B) 4   C) 8   D) 12

    11. A

12. If the sum of the ones' digits is odd, then the whole sum is odd.

    A) $1248 + 8421 = $ ***9   B) $8412 + 4812 = $ ****4
    C) $8421 + 4821 = $ ****2   D) $1248 + 1284 = $ ***2

    12. A

Go on to the next page ⮕ **4**

13. The product of 1 and 19 is 19. The sum of 1 and 19 is 20. A) 12 B) 17 C) 20 D) 28	13. C
14. The tens' digit of 2003×2004 is the same as that of $3 \times 4 = 12$. A) 3 B) 2 C) 1 D) 0	14. C
15. Since "i" comes after "a" in the alphabet, my name could *not* be Simba. A) Simba B) Simbo C) Simbu D) Simby	15. A
16. $36 \div 3 = 12 = 3 \times 4$. A) 33 B) 12 C) 6 D) 4	16. D
17. By working for 7 days from 7 P.M. to 10 P.M., this babysitter worked 7×3 hrs. = 21 hrs. and earned $21 \times \$6 = \$126$. A) \$18 B) \$42 C) \$72 D) \$126	17. D
18. $10 \times 1 \times 11 \times 1 \times 10 = 11 \times 1 \times 1 \times 10 \times 10 = 11 \times 100$. A) 3 B) 10 C) 20 D) 100	18. D
19. Of the numbers 1, 2, 3, 4, 5, 6, 7, 8, and 9, only 3, 6, and 9 are divisible by 3. These are the 3 that are divisible by 3. A) 1 B) 2 C) 3 D) 4	19. C
20. The taxi began with 6 kids. After 3 stops, 3 kids got in the taxi and 6 got out. After 3 stops, there were $6+3-6$ kids = 3 kids in the taxi. A) 3 B) 6 C) 9 D) 12	20. A
21. $4 \times 4 \times 4 = 64 = 8 \times 8$. A) 6×6 B) 8×8 C) 12×12 D) 16×16	21. B
22. (The # of mins. in 1 hr.) − (the # of hrs. in 1 day) = $60 - 24 = 36$. This is 24 less than the number of secs. in 1 min., which is 60. A) 36 less than B) 24 less than C) 24 more than D) 36 more than	22. B
23. In a circle, 1 diameter = 2 radii; so, $4 \times$ diameter = $8 \times$ radius. A) 2 B) π C) 8 D) 16	23. C

Go on to the next page ⏩ **4**

24. My age plus my dog's age was 18 years. Now, each of us is 8 years older. The sum of our current ages is $18 + 8 + 8 = 34$.

    A) 26   B) 34   C) 36   D) 52

    24.
    B

25. Multiples of 4 are $4, 8, \ldots, 92, 96$. To count the numbers on this list, divide 99 by 4 and drop the remainder. Finally, $99 \div 4 = 24+$ remainder.

    A) 20   B) 21   C) 24   D) 25

    25.
    C

26. If the sum of three of the four sides of the square is 18, the length of each side is $18 \div 3 = 6$. The perimeter is $4 \times 6 = 24$.

    A) 6   B) 24   C) 36   D) 72

    26.
    B

27. Each number is its own largest even divisor. Pick the largest #.

    A) 888   B) 6666   C) 44 444   D) 222 222

    27.
    D

28. Of 7 tuba players, 4 play in the orchestra and 7 play in the marching band. Every tuba player plays in the band, so 4 tuba players play in both the orchestra and the band.

    A) 4   B) 6   C) 7   D) 11

    28.
    A

29. The number of ones used in each product is shown below.

    A) 80 too small   B) $88 = 2+2+2+2+5 + (75 \times 1)$; least possible #
    C) $90 = 4+4+5 + (77 \times 1)$ D) $96 = 8+10 + (78 \times 1)$

    29.
    A

30. There are 9 triangles whose sides have length 1. There are 3 triangles whose sides have length 2. There is 1 triangle whose sides have length 3. There are a total of $9 + 3 + 1 = 13$ triangles.

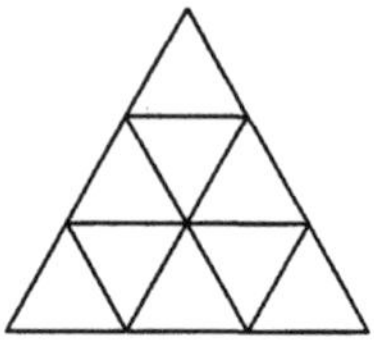

    A) 10   B) 11   C) 12   D) 13

    30.
    D

The end of the contest 🖎 **4**

Visit our Web site at http://www.mathleague.com

FOURTH GRADE MATHEMATICS CONTEST

Math League Press, P.O. Box 17, Tenafly, New Jersey 07670-0017

Information & Solutions

Spring, 2005

Contest Information

4

- **Solutions** Turn the page for detailed contest solutions (written in the question boxes) and letter answers (written in the *Answer Column* to the right of each question).

- **Scores** Please remember that *this is a contest, not a test*—and there is no "passing" or "failing" score. Few students score as high as 24 points (80% correct). Students with half that, 12 points, *deserve commendation!*

- **Answers & Rating Scale** Turn to page 141 for the letter answers to each question and the rating scale for this contest.

1. I can change my \$1 into 10 dimes. Each gumball costs 1 dime. A) 2 B) 5 C) 10 D) 20	1. C
2. If 0 is a factor, the value of the product is 0. A) 0 B) 10 C) 100 D) 2005	2. A
3. Ork the stork delivers 2 babies every day. In 7 days, Ork delivers $2 \times 7 = 14$ babies. A) 2 B) 7 C) 14 D) 21	3. C
4. 2 more than 52 is 54, and 5 less than that is 49. A) 47 B) 49 C) 54 D) 57	4. B
5. One day before Mon. is Sun., so two days before Mon. is Sat. A) Saturday B) Sunday C) Wednesday D) Friday	5. A
6. $(15-14)+(13-12)+(11-10)+(9-8)+(7-6)+(5-4) = 6 \times 1 = 6.$ A) 6 B) 7 C) 12 D) 114	6. A
7. $45 = 15+30$, 15 mins. after 4:45 is 5:00, & 30 mins. later is 5:30. A) 4:00 B) 5:00 C) 5:15 D) 5:30	7. D
8. $\$2 + 20¢ = \$1 + \$1 + 20¢ = \$1 + 100¢ + 20¢ = \$1 + 120¢.$ A) 100 B) 120 C) 200 D) 220	8. B
9. $(205 \times 205) \div 205 = 205 \times (205 \div 205) = 205 \times 1 = 205.$ A) 1 B) 2 C) 25 D) 205	9. D
10. A small wheel on my wheelchair has a diameter that's 16 cm long. This wheel's radius is half as long, 8 cm. A) 4 B) 8 C) 32 D) 196	10. B
11. $1 \times (2 + 3) \times 4 = 1 \times 5 \times 4 = 20.$ A) 10 B) 14 C) 20 D) 24	11. C
12. Ten thousand is written as 10 000. The number of 0s needed is 4. A) 3 B) 4 C) 5 D) 6	12. B

Go on to the next page ⚫⚫⚫▶ **4**

13. $60 \times 60 = 3 \times 20 \times 3 \times 20 = 20 \times 20 \times 3 \times 3 = 20 \times 20 \times 9.$

    A) 3   B) 9   C) 80   D) 900

13. B

14. Use trial and error. If we each put in 4 dimes, then the total number of dimes used would have been $4 \times 4 + 3 = 16 + 3 = 19$. If we each put in 5 dimes, the total would have been $4 \times 5 + 3 = 23$, choice A.

    A) 23   B) 24   C) 25   D) 26

14. A

15. $(8-3) \times (2-1) = (5) \times (1) = 5.$

    A) 1   B) 3   C) 5   D) 9

15. C

16. Since 6633 is *not* even, it *cannot* be divisible by 6.

    A) 3366   B) 4422   C) 6630   D) 6633

16. D

17. When I multiply a number by 5 and the product is 0, then the number itself is 0. When I multiply 0 by 6, that product is also 0.

    A) 0   B) 1   C) 6   D) 12

17. A

18. $(10 \times 100) + (100 \times 10) = 1000 + 1000 = 2000 = 2000$ ones.

    A) 1000   B) 2000   C) 10 000   D) 20 000

18. B

19. The perimeter of my square hammock is 64. Each side of my hammock is $64 \div 4 = 16$.

    A) 4   B) 8   C) 16   D) 32

19. C

20. As shown here, ▢▢ , I can form triangles or rectangles, both of which are polygons.

    A) triangles   B) rectangles
    C) polygons   D) squares

20. D

21. Neither 4 nor 16 is divisible by 12, but 24 is divisible by 8 and 12.

    A) 4   B) 16   C) 24   D) 48

21. C

22. The product of *any* two odd numbers is *always* odd.

    A) 2005   B) even   C) odd   D) prime

22. C

Go on to the next page ⮕ **4**

23. The two whole numbers are 1 and 7. Their sum is $1+7 = 8$.

A) 6   B) 7   C) 8   D) 14

23.

C

24. As you can see from the solution to problem 23, one of the numbers must be 1.

A) 1   B) 2   C) 3   D) 4

24.

A

25. Of the 25 letters besides U, 5 (V, W, X, Y, and Z) come after U, and $25-5 = 20$ letters come before.

A) E   B) G   C) T   D) U

25.

D

26. Since $37¢-22¢ = 15¢$, doubling my nickels gave me 3 nickels' worth more. So I must have had 3 nickels before doubling.

A) 3   B) 4   C) 5   D) 6

26.

A

27. 12 clips for 48¢ = 1 for 4¢. For \$1, I get $100¢÷4¢ = 25$ paper clips.

A) 24   B) 25   C) 26   D) 96

27.

B

28. Sam bought twice as many ice pops as Lee. Since Sam bought 18, Lee bought 9. Lee bought 3 times as many as Pat. Since Lee bought 9, Pat bought 3.

A) 1   B) 3   C) 6   D) 9

28.

B

29. If the bus & train are on the same side, one 2 km and one 5 km from the vendor, then the distance between the bus and train is $(5-2)$ km = 3 km.

A) 3 km   B) 5 km   C) 7 km   D) 10 km

29.

A

30. My sunflower doubles in size 6 times: First it's 2 times, then 4 times, 8 times, 16 times, 32 times, and finally 64 times as big.

A) 2   B) 6   C) 49   D) 64

30.

D

The end of the contest **4**

Visit our web site at http://www.mathleague.com

Information & Solutions

Spring, 2006

Contest Information

4

- **Solutions** Turn the page for detailed contest solutions (written in the question boxes) and letter answers (written in the *Answer Column* to the right of each question).

- **Scores** Please remember that *this is a contest, not a test*—and there is no "passing" or "failing" score. Few students score as high as 24 points (80% correct). Students with half that, 12 points, *deserve commendation!*

- **Answers & Rating Scale** Turn to page 142 for the letter answers to each question and the rating scale for this contest.

1. I had 300¢. I spent 3¢. The amount I have left is 297¢ = \$2.97. A) \$2.70 B) \$2.93 C) \$2.97 D) \$3.03	1. C
2. If any factor is 0, the product is 0. A) 0 B) 26 C) 120 D) 2006	2. A
3. My teacher pointed to a square board whose perimeter is 24. The length of one side of the square is $24 \div 4 = 6$. A) 4 B) 6 C) 8 D) 20	3. B
4. $36 \div 3 = 12$, and $12 = 4 \times 3$. A) 12 B) 9 C) 8 D) 3	4. D
5. $5600 - 5555 = 45$ and $5555 - 5500 = 55$, so 5555 is closer to 5600. A) 5600 B) 5560 C) 5550 D) 5500	5. A
6. $(10-9) + (8-7) + (6-5) + (4-3) + (2-1) = 1+1+1+1+1 = 5$. A) 10 B) 7 C) 6 D) 5	6. D
7. Each horse needs 2 pairs; so we'll need $14 \times 2 = 28$ pairs. A) 7 B) 14 C) 28 D) 56	7. C
8. $8 \times 4 = 32 = 2 \times 4 \times 4$. A) 2 B) 4 C) 8 D) 16	8. B
9. $(70 + 50 + 60) - (50 + 60 + 70) = 0$. A) 70 B) 40 C) 30 D) 0	9. D
10. 2 hrs. = 2×60 mins. = 120 mins. = 6×20 mins., so it takes grandpa 6 days to ride my horse for 2 hours. A) 3 B) 4 C) 6 D) 10	10. C
11. $900 + 90 + 99 = 1089$. A) 9999 B) 1089 C) 999 D) 989	11. B
12. Tomorrow is Saturday (3 days before Tuesday); so today is Friday. A) Friday B) Saturday C) Sunday D) Thursday	12. A

Go on to the next page ⟹ **4**

13. It rained on the 1st, 3rd, 5th, . . . , 31st. That's 16 days. A) 15 B) 16 C) 29 D) 31	13. B
14. $8 weighs 200 g, $4 weighs 100 g, $2 weighs 50 g, and $1 weighs 25 g. Now, triple: $3 weighs 75 g. A) 50 g B) 60 g C) 75 g D) 80 g	14. C
15. Note that $1 \times 2 \times 3 \times 4 \times 5 = 120$, but $12 \times 15 = 180$. A) 12×15 B) 6×20 C) 24×5 D) 30×4	15. A
16. $36 = 16+20$, so $36+36+36$ has 3 extra 20s. A) 20 B) 30 C) 40 D) 60	16. D
17. Since 20 nickels is $1 and 20 dimes is $2, the total number of coins is 40. A) 60 B) 40 C) 30 D) 20	17. B
18. $64+64+64 = 192 = 8 \times 24$. A) 8 B) 12 C) 16 D) 24	18. D
19. The perimeter of the shaded region is the perimeter of the larger square + the perimeter of the smaller square $= 32 + 16 = 48$. A) 48 B) 36 C) 32 D) 16	19. A
20. $1 + 8 + 27 + 64 = 100 = 10 \times 10$. A) 10×10 B) 12×34 C) $1+4+9+16$ D) $12+34$	20. A
21. The number 48 has 10 factors: 1, 2, 3, 4, 6, 8, 12, 16, 24, 48. A) 38 B) 48 C) 58 D) 68	21. B
22. Between them are the 10th, 11th, . . . , 26th people in line. If you wrote down all these numbers, your list would have 17 numbers. A) 16 B) 17 C) 18 D) 19	22. B
23. If 2 whole numbers differ by 2, their product *cannot* be 105. A) 3×5 B) 5×7 C) 7×15 D) 13×15	23. C

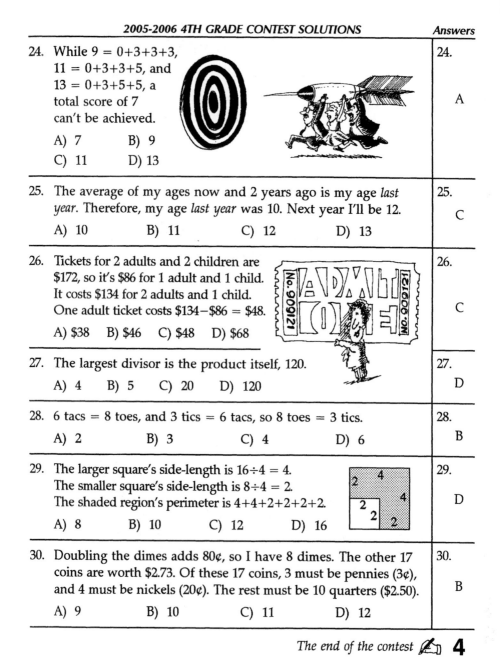

24. While 9 = 0+3+3+3,
    11 = 0+3+3+5, and
    13 = 0+3+5+5, a
    total score of 7
    can't be achieved.

    A) 7   B) 9
    C) 11   D) 13

24.

A

25. The average of my ages now and 2 years ago is my age *last year*. Therefore, my age *last year* was 10. Next year I'll be 12.

    A) 10   B) 11   C) 12   D) 13

25.

C

26. Tickets for 2 adults and 2 children are $172, so it's $86 for 1 adult and 1 child. It costs $134 for 2 adults and 1 child. One adult ticket costs $134−$86 = $48.

    A) $38   B) $46   C) $48   D) $68

26.

C

27. The largest divisor is the product itself, 120.

    A) 4   B) 5   C) 20   D) 120

27.

D

28. 6 tacs = 8 toes, and 3 tics = 6 tacs, so 8 toes = 3 tics.

    A) 2   B) 3   C) 4   D) 6

28.

B

29. The larger square's side-length is 16÷4 = 4. The smaller square's side-length is 8÷4 = 2. The shaded region's perimeter is 4+4+2+2+2+2.

    A) 8   B) 10   C) 12   D) 16

29.

D

30. Doubling the dimes adds 80¢, so I have 8 dimes. The other 17 coins are worth $2.73. Of these 17 coins, 3 must be pennies (3¢), and 4 must be nickels (20¢). The rest must be 10 quarters ($2.50).

    A) 9   B) 10   C) 11   D) 12

30.

B

The end of the contest ✍ **4**

Visit our Web site at http://www.mathleague.com

5th Grade Solutions

2001-2002 through 2005-2006

Information & Solutions

Spring, 2002

Contest Information

5

- **Solutions** Turn the page for detailed contest solutions (written in the question boxes) and letter answers (written in the *Answer Column* to the right of each question).

- **Scores** Please remember that *this is a contest, not a test*—and there is no "passing" or "failing" score. Few students score as high as 24 points (80% correct). Students with half that, 12 points, *deserve commendation!*

- **Answers & Rating Scale** Turn to page 143 for the letter answers to each question and the rating scale for this contest.

95

	Answers
1. $30 + 31 + 32 = (29+1) + (30+1) + (31+1) = 29 + 30 + 31 + 3.$ A) 0 B) 1 C) 2 D) 3	1. D
2. $(3\times4\times5\times6)\div15 = [(3\times5)\times(4\times6)]\div15 = [15\times(24)]\div15 = 24.$ A) 8 B) 10 C) 12 D) 24	2. D
3. Don't count the first 5 people or the last person on line, a total of 6 people. That leaves a total of $44-6 = 38$ people. A) 34 B) 38 C) 39 D) 49	3. B
4. $7\times1+7\times2+7\times3 = 7\times(1+2+3) = 7\times6.$ A) 6 B) 5 C) 4 D) 3	4. A
5. 20 hundreds + 2 ones = $20\times100 + 2\times1 = 2000 + 2 = 2002.$ A) 202 B) 222 C) 2002 D) 2020	5. C
6. Each book is shared by 2 students, so 40 need $40 \div 2 = 20$ books. A) 20 books B) 40 books C) 60 books D) 80 books	6. A
7. To climb 300 trees, at 12 trees per day, I need $300\div12 = 25$ days. A) 12 B) 20 C) 25 D) 36	7. C
8. $45 \div 3 = 15 = 3\times5.$ A) 20 B) 15 C) 10 D) 5	8. D
9. Of Early Bird's 36 worms, 3 times as many were fat as were thin. Split the 36 worms into 4 piles of 9 worms. Put fat worms in 3 of the piles. There are $3\times9 = 27$ fat worms. A) 9 B) 24 C) 27 D) 30	9. C
10. Since $180 \div 3 = 60 = 3\times 20$, it's the one that's a multiple of 3. A) $120 \div 3$ B) $150 \div 3$ C) $180 \div 3$ D) $210 \div 3$	10. C
11. $48 = 1\times48 = 2\times24 = 3\times16 = 4\times12 = 6\times8.$ The product of 4 and 12 is 48, their difference is 8, and their sum is $4 + 12 = 16.$ A) 12 B) 16 C) 18 D) 24	11. B

Go on to the next page ⟫ **5**

12. 1 day + (24 + 24 + 12) hours = 3 days + 12 hours A) 1 B) 12 C) 20 D) 24	12. B
13. There were as many kids in the first car of the roller coaster as the largest possible sum of two different one-digit numbers. There were 9+8 = 17 kids. A) 16 B) 17 C) 18 D) 19	13. B
14. Any number with a factor of 0 is equal to 0. A) 100 000×0 B) 1000×1000 C) 100×1000 D) 10×10 000	14. A
15. (# of sides of a triangle)×(# of sides of an octagon) = 3×8 = 24 = 4×6 = (# of sides of a square)×(# of sides of a *hexagon*). A) triangle B) rectangle C) pentagon D) hexagon	15. D
16. Easiest way: each of the pairs (1,39), (9,31), (11,29), (19,21) averages 20. A) 19 B) 20 C) 21 D) 40	16. B
17. Value of 12 = 12×25¢ = $3 < $12 = value of 120 dimes. A) 3 dollars B) 60 nickels C) 120 dimes D) 300 pennies	17. C
18. A triangle, the polygon with the fewest sides, has 3 sides. A) 1 B) 2 C) 3 D) 4	18. C
19. 9999 ÷ 99 = 101; 99 less than that is 101 − 99 = 2. A) 0 B) 2 C) 200 D) 9999	19. B
20. Use just the ones' digits. Since 9×9×9 = 729, the answer is 9. A) 9 B) 7 C) 3 D) 1	20. A
21. In 8 hrs = 480 mins = ten 48-minute periods, I'll eat (18×12)×10 = 2160 bowls. A) 108 B) 180 C) 216 D) 2160	21. D
22. 1000÷7 leaves remainder 6; so 994÷7 leaves remainder 0, and 9+9+4 = 22. A) 7 B) 18 C) 21 D) 22	22. D

Go on to the next page Ⅲ➡ **5**

97

23. 1 dime + 3 nickels = 25¢, 2 dimes + 4 nickels = 40¢, and 3 dimes + 5 nickels = 55¢. The value *cannot* be choice D.

    A) 25¢   B) 40¢   C) 55¢   D) 75¢

    23.

    D

24. The 2002nd even number is 2 × 2002. Subtract 1.

    A) 4001   B) 4003   C) 4004   D) 4005

    24.

    B

25. A square has 4 sides. *Both* pairs of its opposite sides are parallel.

    A) 4   B) 3   C) 2   D) 1

    25.

    C

26. Since 20 letters appear before the letter "U," and 5 letters appear after it, the correct answer is choice D.

    A) E   B) F   C) T   D) U

    26.

    D

27. In a magic square, the sum of the numbers in each row, column, and major diagonal is called the *magic sum*. To increase the sum of each row, column, and diagonal by a total of 15, increase each of the 3 numbers added by 15÷3 = 5.

    | 4 | 9 | 2 |
    | 3 | 5 | 7 |
    | 8 | 1 | 6 |

    A) 5   B) 7   C) 8   D) 15

    27.

    A

28. The possible products are 6, 7, 8, 9, 10, 12, 14, 16, 18, 20, 21, 24, 27, 28, 30, 32, 35, 36, 40, 45, 50. There are 21 different products. The 4 duplicates are 6×3 = 9×2, 6×4 = 8×3, 3×10 = 5×6, and 4×10 = 5×8.

    A) 5   B) 10   C) 21   D) 25

    28.

    C

29. The quotient 189 ÷ 15 has a remainder of 9, not 3.

    A) 15   B) 31   C) 62   D) 186

    29.

    A

30. Each of the 300 students in my school played miniature golf exactly 2 of the past 5 nights. Average # of students per night, over 5 nights = (300×2)÷5 = 120.

    A) 100   B) 120   C) 150   D) 600

    30.

    B

The end of the contest ☞ **5**

Visit our web site at http://www.mathleague.com

Information & Solutions

Spring, 2003

Contest Information

5

- **Solutions** Turn the page for detailed contest solutions (written in the question boxes) and letter answers (written in the *Answer Column* to the right of each question).

- **Scores** Please remember that *this is a contest, not a test*—and there is no "passing" or "failing" score. Few students score as high as 24 points (80% correct). Students with half that, 12 points, *deserve commendation!*

- **Answers & Rating Scale** Turn to page 144 for the letter answers to each question and the rating scale for this contest.

	Answers

1. $14+15+16-(4+5+6) = (14-4)+(15-5)+(16-6) = 10+10+10 = 30.$
   A) 7   B) 10   C) 20   D) 30

1. D

2. $1\times25¢ + 2\times10¢ + 3\times5¢ + 4\times1¢ = 25¢+20¢+15¢+4¢ = 64¢.$
   A) 41¢   B) 64¢   C) 75¢   D) $1.41

2. B

3. My sea serpent, 39 m long, painted rings, each 3 m wide, on its body. That's at most $39\div3 = 13$ rings.
   A) 3   B) 9
   C) 13   D) 117

3. C

4. $(2\times4\times6\times8) \div 32 = (2\times6\times32)\div32 = 2\times6.$ A) 6   B) 8   C) 10   D) 12

4. D

5. Eating 3 each hour, in 24 hours he eats 3×24 bags = 72 bags.
   A) 8 bags   B) 21 bags   C) 27 bags   D) 72 bags

5. D

6. The quotient $42 \div 2 = 21$ equals the product $3\times7 = 21$.
   A) 3×6 B) 3×7 C) 3×14 D) 3×21

6. B

7. I own 16 leashes. I must own 8 dogs, since $16 \div 2 = 8$.
   A) 8   B) 16   C) 17   D) 32

7. A

8. $800 - 80 = 720.$ A) 820   B) 792   C) 720   D) 700

8. C

9. # sides: A) 6 sides   B) no sides   C) 5 sides   D) 3 sides.
   A) hexagon   B) circle   C) pentagon   D) triangle

9. A

10. Since 150 4th graders need 3 buses, 200 5th graders need 4 buses, and 250 6th graders need 5 buses, we need $3+4+5 = 12$ buses.
    A) 3   B) 7   C) 9   D) 12

10. D

11. $(2\times4)+(3\times4)+(4\times4)+(5\times4) = (2+3+4+5)\times4.$
    A) 8   B) 14   C) 20   D) 120

11. B

12. 31 days before June 1 is May 1; 29 days before May 1 is April 2.
    A) March 31   B) April 1
    C) April 2   D) April 3

12. C

13. Since $135\div45 = 3$, it follows that $136\div45$ is greater than 3.
    A) $162\div54 = 3$ B) $174\div87 = 2$ C) $186\div63 < 3$ D) $136\div45 > 3$

13. D

Go on to the next page ⏵ **5**

14. The 10 thousands' digit of 987 654 is 8; 1 less than 8 is $8-1 = 7$.

    A) 4   B) 5   C) 7   D) 8

14.
C

15. The average value of my 5 heart sculptures is $\$2 \div 5 = 200¢ \div 5 = 40¢$.

    A) 4¢   B) 10¢
    C) $10   D) 40¢

15.
D

16. $3 \times 20 \times 100 = 3 \times 10 \times 2 \times 100 = 30 \times (2 \times 100)$.

    A) 2×100 B) 2×10 C) 20×100 D) 200×100

16.
A

17. If a diameter is 6 m long, a radius is (6 m) $\div 2 = 3$ m long.

    A) 3 m   B) 6 m   C) 12 m   D) 18 m

17.
A

18. $80 \times 1 = 80 = 80 \div 1$. (*Note:* No number may be divided by 0.)

    A) 0   B) 1   C) 2   D) 80

18.
B

19. 8 hrs. before 7:07 P.M. is 11:07 A.M.; 8 mins. earlier is 10:59 A.M.

    A) 3:15 A.M.   B) 5:15 A.M.   C) 9:59 A.M.   D) 10:59 A.M.

19.
D

20. There are 12 girls and 18 boys in my class.

    A) 12   B) 18   C) 20   D) 24

20.
B

21. $111 \times 444 = 49284$; the product has only one odd digit, the 9.

    A) zero   B) one   C) three   D) nine

21.
B

22. The board has $9 \times 9 = 81$ squares in all. If there were an even number of squares, half would be dark. Since the 81 squares alternate in color, at most 41 are of either color.

    A) 38   B) 39   C) 40   D) 41

22.
D

23. Ted turned 10 years old yesterday. Averaging his ages on his 5 most recent birthdays, I get $(6+7+8+9+10) \div 5 = 8$.

    A) 6   B) 7   C) 8   D) 9

23.
C

Go on to the next page ▥➡ **5**

24. Since one of the factors is 10, the product's ones' digit is a 0. A) 2 B) 4 C) 8 D) 0	24. D
25. All 66 gloves are black or blue. If twice as many are black as are blue, my mom has 44 black and 22 blue gloves. The number of pairs of blue gloves is $22 \div 2 = 11$. A) 11 B) 22 C) 44 D) 132	25. A
26. Half the 60 coins are nickels; one-third are dimes. The 20 dimes are worth $2.00. The 30 nickels are worth only $1.50, which is 50¢ less. A) 50¢ less B) 50¢ more C) 10¢ less D) 10¢ more	26. A
27. Al's plant had 10 flowers at first. Since 8 wilted, only 2 of the original flowers remain. In place of the 8 that wilted are $8 \times 2 = 16$ new flowers. In all, he has $2 + 16 = 18$ flowers. A) 16 B) 18 C) 20 D) 26	27. B
28. Without lifting your pencil or folding the paper, it's not possible to draw a path connecting points X and Y without crossing the curve. As shown by the dotted path, X and A can be connected without crossing the curve. A) A B) B C) C D) D	28. A
29. In 60 minutes, I burp $6 \times 3 = 18$ times and you burp $5 \times 4 = 20$ times. Altogether, we burp $18 + 20 = 38$ times every 60 minutes, or 19 times every 30. A) 7, 22 B) 11, 15 C) 13, 20 D) 19, 30	29. D
30. The area of the room is (20×30) m^2 = 600 m^2. The dimensions of the unpainted part are 16 by 26, so its area is 416 m^2. The area of the strip is $(600 - 416)$ m^2 = 184 m^2. A) 96 m^2 B) 100 m^2 C) 184 m^2 D) 200 m^2	30. C

The end of the contest ✍ **5**

Visit our Web site at http://www.mathleague.com

Information & Solutions

Spring, 2004

Contest Information

5

- **Solutions** Turn the page for detailed contest solutions (written in the question boxes) and letter answers (written in the *Answer Column* to the right of each question).

- **Scores** Please remember that *this is a contest, not a test*—and there is no "passing" or "failing" score. Few students score as high as 24 points (80% correct). Students with half that, 12 points, *deserve commendation!*

- **Answers & Rating Scale** Turn to page 145 for the letter answers to each question and the rating scale for this contest.

1. Go backwards: Wednesday, Tuesday, Monday (the answer).

   A) Monday   B) Tuesday   C) Saturday   D) Sunday

2. $2+12+22 = (1+1) + (11+1) + (21+1) = 1+11+21 + 3.$

   A) 1   B) 2   C) 3   D) 4

3. My lunch costs me
   $10 \times 5\text{¢} + 10 \times 10\text{¢} = 50\text{¢} + 100\text{¢} = \$1.50.$

   A) \$1.10   B) \$1.20   C) \$1.50   D) \$2

4. $(45 \div 5)+(36 \div 4)+(27 \div 3) = 9+9+9 = 9 \times 3.$

   A) 1   B) 3   C) 6   D) 12

5. Since $27 \times 3 = 3 \times 27$, the correct answer is choice A.

   A) 3   B) 9   C) 81   D) 243

6. $6+12+18+24+30 = 6+24 + 12+18 + 30 = 30+30+30 = 90 = 6 \times 15.$

   A) 10   B) 12   C) 13   D) 15

7. $10 \times 10 = 100 = 1000 \div 10$, so choice B is correct.

   A) $100 \div 10$ B) $1000 \div 10$ C) $100 \div 100$ D) $1000 \div 100$

8. The product of 0 and any number is 0, so the product is 0.

   A) 0   B) 100   C) 240   D) 12 100

9. The rear wheel costs \$4 more. Split the
   remaining \$22-\$4 = \$18 cost equally.
   The front wheel costs half of \$18 = \$9.

   A) 18   B) 13   C) 11   D) 9

10. Each time I go on both rides once, I
    need 5 tickets. To go on both rides 5
    times, I will need $5 \times 5 = 25$ tickets.

    A) 5   B) 10   C) 25   D) 30

11. Since $54 320 + 54 321 = 108 641$, the sum has 6 digits.

    A) 5   B) 6   C) 10   D) 11

Go on to the next page ⫸ **5**

12. $7 + (7-7) + (7-7) + 7 = 14$. A) 0 B) 7 C) 14 D) 21	12. C
13. 300 minutes = 5 hours, so I'll travel 5×30 km = 150 km. A) 10 km B) 15 km C) 100 km D) 150 km	13. D
14. Juan is 20 years old now. In 20 years, his age will be 40. A) 10 B) 20 C) 30 D) 40	14. D
15. The fish weighed 120 kg, which is 3 times as much as I weigh. I weigh $(120\,\text{kg}) \div 3 = 40\,\text{kg}$. A) 30 B) 40 C) 60 D) 360	15. B
16. $(3 \times 3) \times (3 \times 3) \times (3 \times 3) = 9 \times 9 \times 9$. A) 9×9 B) $9+9$ C) $9 \times 9 \times 9$ D) $9+9+9$	16. C
17. By definition, the only positive factors of a *prime* number are itself and 1. A) prime B) odd C) even D) composite	17. A
18. Of 9, 70, 500, 3000, the largest is 3000. A) 9 ones B) 7 tens C) 5 hundreds D) 3 thousands	18. D
19. $(4 \times \text{length of one side}) \div (\text{length of one side}) = 4$. A) 1 B) 2 C) 4 D) 16	19. C
20. Try the choices. If Baby is 3, twice Baby's age is 6. Then, 3 times Baby's age 1 hour ago $= 3 \times 2 = 6$, so they are equal. A) 2 B) 3 C) 4 D) 6	20. B
21. $9 \div 9 = 1$, and 1 is *not* divisible by 9. A) $9-9$ B) $9+9$ C) 9×9 D) $9 \div 9$	21. D
22. There are 5 "twenties" with an even tens' digit: 21, 23, 25, 27, 29. There are also 5 "forties," 5 "sixties," and 5 "eighties," 20 in all. A) 20 B) 22 C) 23 D) 25	22. A

Go on to the next page ‖▶ **5**

23. Divide 130 by 8. The quotient is 16 and the remainder is 2. My favorite number is 16. The sum of the digits of 16 is $1 + 6 = 7$.

    A) 6   B) 7   C) 8   D) 9

    23. B

24. There are 5, 6, 7, or 8 friends. Now divide $88.92 by each. The only division in which the remainder is 0 is $88.92 \div 6 = \$14.82$.

    A) $17.78   B) $14.82
    C) $12.70   D) $11.12

    24. B

25. Since 10 dimes = $1, then 250 dimes is 25 times as much, or $25. None of the other choices gives a whole number of dollars.

    A) dimes   B) nickels   C) pennies   D) quarters

    25. A

26. If each of the numbers 2, 4, 8, and 16 is increased by 2, then there are 4 increases of 2, and the total increase is $4 \times 2 = 8$.

    A) 2   B) 4   C) 8   D) 16

    26. C

27. The letter L is formed by 2 line segments. Of the letters shown below, C is curved, F is formed by 3 line segments, H by 3 line segments, and V (the answer) by 2 line segments.

    A) C   B) F   C) H   D) V

    27. D

28. Ballet Bear can do 72 pirouettes in 12 minutes. This is $72 \div 12 = 6$ pirouettes each minute. In 3 minutes, Ballet Bear can do $6 \times 3 = 18$ pirouettes.

    A) 6   B) 12   C) 18   D) 24

    28. C

29. Since 4 is already a multiple of 2, the l.c.m. of 1, 2, 3, 4, 5 is $3 \times 4 \times 5 = 60$.

    A) 720   B) 360   C) 120   D) 60

    29. D

30. If the length of each side of a rectangle is a whole number, its perimeter = $2\ell + 2w$ is divisible by 2, but not equal to 2.

    A) triangle   B) hexagon   C) pentagon   D) rectangle

    30. D

The end of the contest 🖊 **5**

Visit our Web site at http://www.mathleague.com

Information & Solutions

Spring, 2005

Contest Information

5

- **Solutions** Turn the page for detailed contest solutions (written in the question boxes) and letter answers (written in the *Answer Column* to the right of each question).

- **Scores** Please remember that *this is a contest, not a test*—and there is no "passing" or "failing" score. Few students score as high as 24 points (80% correct). Students with half that, 12 points, *deserve commendation!*

- **Answers & Rating Scale** Turn to page 146 for the letter answers to each question and the rating scale for this contest.

1. $(100+100)+(200+100)+(300+100) = 100+200+300+300.$

   A) 100   B) 200   C) 300   D) 400

   1.
   C

2. Two-dozen truckloads of dirt = $2 \times 12 = 24$ truckloads. Two fewer than that is $24-2 = 22$ truckloads.

   A) 10   B) 12   C) 20   D) 22

   2.
   D

3. $27 \div 3 = 9$, and $9 = 3 \times 3$.

   A) 3   B) 6   C) 9   D) 27

   3.
   A

4. For each coin that lands tails up, two land heads up. Make a list. Look for a sum of 9: $1t,2h$; $2t,4h$; $3t,6h$. Finally, $3+6 = 9$.

   A) 3   B) 4   C) 5   D) 6

   4.
   D

5. 19 tens $-$ 19 ones = $(19 \times 10)-(19 \times 1) = 190-19 = 171$.

   A) 1871   B) 342   C) 171   D) 9

   5.
   C

6. $4 \times 8 \times 12 = 4 \times (4 \times 2) \times 12 = (4 \times 4) \times (2 \times 12) = 16 \times 24.$

   A) 32   B) 24   C) 20   D) 16

   What's up?

   6.
   B

7. My neck, which grows 5 cm in 10 days, grows $10 \times 5 = 50$ cm in $10 \times 10 = 100$ days.

   A) 5   B) 10   C) 25   D) 100

   7.
   D

8. $(33+44+55+66) \div 11 = 3+4+5+6 = 18.$

   A) 18   B) 11   C) 9   D) 7

   8.
   A

9. Even numbers divisible by 3 are divisible by 6.

   A) 166   B) 266   C) 366   D) 466

   9.
   C

10. Pete got $3.60 in change, so 4 frozen pizzas cost Pete 20.00-$$3.60 = \$16.40$. One frozen pizza cost Pete $\$16.40 \div 4 = \$4.10$.

    A) $4.10   B) $5   C) $6.25   D) $9

    10.
    A

11. $(48 \times 2) + (48 \times 3) + (48 \times 4) = 48 \times (2 + 3 + 4) = 48 \times 9.$

    A) 24   B) 9   C) 5   D) 3

    11.
    B

Go on to the next page ⟫ **5**

		Answers
12.	The ratio (4 side-lengths) ÷ (2 side-lengths) = 4÷2 = 2. A) 1 B) 2 C) 4 D) 8	12. B
13.	Four years ago, Tom was 8. Six years ago, he was 6. The average of 8 and 6 is 7. A) 11 B) 7 C) 5 D) 4	13. B
14.	12 hours before noon is 12 midnight. 12 minutes before 12 midnight is 11:48 P.M. I was wandering around at 11:48 P.M. A) 11:48 A.M. B) 12:12 A.M. C) 11:48 P.M. D) 12:12 P.M.	14. C
15.	Two million = 2 000 000 = 2000 × 1000. A) 200 × 100 B) 200 × 1000 C) 2000 × 1000 D) 20 000 × 10	15. C
16.	The *greatest* 3-digit number is 999, and the *greatest* 4-digit number is 9999. Their sum is 999 + 9999 = 10 998. A) 9998 B) 9999 C) 10 000 D) 10 998	16. D
17.	The ape ate 6 bananas daily. It ate 5×6 = 30 bananas in 5 days. A) 20 B) 24 C) 30 D) 120	17. C
18.	Every side of the triangle is 6 cm long. The triangle's perimeter is 6+6+6 = 18 cm. A) 2 B) 6 C) 18 D) 36	18. C
19.	First 6 months take about 6×30 = 180 days, so day 199 falls in month 7, July. A) May B) June C) July D) August	19. C
20.	When 728 is divided by 72, the remainder is 8. A) 7 B) 8 C) 28 D) 72	20. D
21.	The product 1111 × 1111 equals 1 234 321. The largest *odd* digit in this product is 3. A) 1 B) 3 C) 4 D) 5	21. B

Go on to the next page IIII➡ **5**

22. Use trial & error. Double each choice to try to get my original #. For *A*, half my # is 3, my # is 6, twice it is 12. The product is 72. A) 3 B) 6 C) 12 D) 36	22. A
23. If Mary got all 100s, her average would have been 100. Since 98 is just a little less than 100, try four 100s and one 90. Finally, $(400+90) \div 5 = 98$, as required. A) 1 B) 2 C) 3 D) 4	23. A
24. Since 121 is divisible by 11, the remainder is 006, or 6. A) 6 B) 5 C) 4 D) 3	24. A
25. The g.c.d. of 6, 16, & 26 is 2, so the g.c.d. of 60, 160, & 260 is 20. A) 5 B) 6 C) 20 D) 60	25. C
26. The middle # is $2005 \div 5 = 401$. The sum of the digits of the 5 #s is $(3+9+9)+(4+0+0)+(4+0+1)+(4+0+2)+(4+0+3) = 43$. A) 15 B) 25 C) 34 D) 43	26. D
27. If 2 splashes = 3 splishes, then (9×2) splashes = (9×3) splishes. A) 12 B) 27 C) 36 D) 48	27. B
28. The smallest such number is 6, and the largest such number is 95. There are 90 whole numbers from 6 through 95. A) 89 B) 90 C) 91 D) 100	28. B
29. The l.c.m. of 6 & 9 is 18. The 5 numbers are 18, 36, 54, 72, & 90. A) 2 B) 3 C) 4 D) 5	29. D
30. $1+3+ \ldots +99 = (2-1)+(4-1)+ \ldots +(100-1) = 2550-50 = 2500$. A) 2400 B) 2450 C) 2500 D) 2550	30. C

The end of the contest **5**

Visit our Web site at http://www.mathleague.com

110

Information & Solutions

Spring, 2006

Contest Information

5

- **Solutions** Turn the page for detailed contest solutions (written in the question boxes) and letter answers (written in the *Answer Column* to the right of each question).

- **Scores** Please remember that *this is a contest, not a test*—and there is no "passing" or "failing" score. Few students score as high as 24 points (80% correct). Students with half that, 12 points, *deserve commendation!*

- **Answers & Rating Scale** Turn to page 147 for the letter answers to each question and the rating scale for this contest.

1. $(9 + 9) + (9 + 9) + 9 = 18 + 18 + 9$.

   A) 0   B) 9   C) 18   D) 36

   1. B

2. It crawls 25 m in 30 mins.; 9 such trips = 225 m in 4 hrs. 30 mins.

   A) 4   B) $4\frac{1}{2}$ C) 5   D) $5\frac{1}{2}$

   2. B

3. A pair is 2, so 12 pairs = $2 \times 12 = 24$ socks.

   A) 6   B) 12   C) 24   D) 48

   3. C

4. The total weight of 7 giant carrots, each weighing 700 g, is 7×700 g $= 4900$ g.

   A) 100   B) 490   C) 700   D) 4900

   4. D

5. $(11+10+1) - (11-10-1) = 22-0 = 22$.

   A) 22   B) 11   C) 10   D) 0

   5. A

6. 10 nickels = 5 dimes, so it's 15 dimes.

   A) pennies   B) nickels
   C) dimes   D) quarters

   6. C

7. Each of the 8 digits in List K is 1 more than the digit below it in List L. The sum is 8 more.

   List K: 3 1 6 9 5 2 8 7

   List L: 2 0 5 8 4 1 7 6

   A) 1   B) 8   C) 33   D) 41

   7. B

8. Since $3 \times 14 = 42$, the quotient $43 \div 14$ is more than $42 \div 14 = 3$.

   A) $30 \div 11$ B) $31 \div 12$ C) $35 \div 12$ D) $43 \div 14$

   8. D

9. 60 mins. = 1 hr, so 3:40 + 20 mins. = 4:00.

   A) 20   B) 30   C) 40   D) 60

   9. A

10. If 6 beavers can clear the trees from a lot in 36 hours, then twice as many beavers (12) will need only half as much time (18 hours) to clear these same trees.

    A) 18   B) 24   C) 54   D) 72

    10. A

11. Each side's length is $24 \div 4 = 6$. The sum for 3 sides is 18.

    A) 6   B) 8   C) 12   D) 18

    11. D

Go on to the next page ▮▮▮➡ **5**

12. Since 20 added to 100 is 120, and $4 \times 30 = 120$, the answer is B. A) 20 $\qquad$ B) 30 $\qquad$ C) 80 $\qquad$ D) 120	12. B
13. In any row or column with 3 numbers, the sum of the 3 numbers is 255. The sum of the 2 numbers already in the third column is $68+136 = 204$. The missing number is $255-204 = 51$. A) 41 $\quad$ B) 49 $\quad$ C) 50 $\quad$ D) 51 $\begin{array}{\|c\|c\|c\|} \hline 34 & 153 & 68 \\ \hline 119 & 85 & \\ \hline 102 & 17 & 136 \\ \hline \end{array}$	13. D
14. Odd+odd = even. Also, the 2 odd numbers must be *different*. A) $2 = 1+1$ $\quad$ B) 3 $\qquad$ C) $4 = 1+3$ $\quad$ D) 5	14. C
15. 5 books have 315 pages each; their total page count is $5 \times 315 = 1575$. The other 6 books have a total of $(2175-1575)$ pages. A) 700 $\qquad$ B) 600 $\qquad$ C) 550 $\qquad$ D) 500	15. B
16. Use subtraction: $6002-2006 = 3996$. A) 3996 $\quad$ B) 4004 $\quad$ C) 4006 $\quad$ D) 8008	16. A
17. Triplets are 3, so 16 triplets = $16 \times 3 = 48$. Twins are 2. Since $48 \div 2 = 24$, the lovebirds' 16 triplets is the same number of birds as there are in 24 sets of twins. A) 4 $\qquad$ B) 8 C) 12 $\qquad$ D) 24	17. D
18. First, twice 24 is 48. That's 3 times the number of pencils you have, so the number of pencils you have is $48 \div 3 = 16$. A) 4 $\qquad$ B) 8 $\qquad$ C) 12 $\qquad$ D) 16	18. D
19. 2 d before yesterday = 3 d before today = 4 d before tomorrow. A) 5 $\qquad$ B) 4 $\qquad$ C) 3 $\qquad$ D) 2	19. B
20. Since $3000 \times 30\,000 = 90\,000\,000$, the product has 1 non-zero digit. A) 1 $\qquad$ B) 2 $\qquad$ C) 3 $\qquad$ D) 9	20. A
21. An octagon has 8 sides. A trapezoid has 4 sides. $2 \times 4 = 8$. A) 1 $\qquad$ B) 2 $\qquad$ C) 3 $\qquad$ D) 4	21. B
22. There are 48 such numbers: $2 \times 2, 2 \times 3, \ldots, 2 \times 48$, and 2×49. A) 48 $\qquad$ B) 49 $\qquad$ C) 50 $\qquad$ D) 98	22. A

Go on to the next page ▐▶ **5**

23.	I paid \$1 for 4 pens, or 25¢ each. You paid 40¢ for 2, or 20¢ each.			23.
	A) 5¢ B) 15¢ C) 20¢ D) 25¢			A

24.	Add 6 years to get twice my age, 30. I'm 15. In 2 years I'll be 17.	24.
	A) 11 B) 15 C) 17 D) 20	C

25. I delivered 3 pink and 2 blue boxes. The total weight of the 3 pink boxes was the same as the total weight of the 2 blue boxes. I delivered 2 blue boxes, so the 5 boxes weigh the same as 2 deliveries of 2 blue boxes each. Thus, 4 blue boxes weigh a total of 60 kg. Each weighs (60 kg)÷4 = 15 kg.

A) 12 kg   B) 15 kg   C) 20 kg   D) 30 kg

25. B

26. $6 \times 7 \times 8 \times 9 \times 10 = (1 \times 2 \times 3)(7)(2 \times 4)(9)(2 \times 5)$ is a multiple of $1 \times 2 \times 3 \times 4 \times 5$, so the remainder is 0.

A) 63   B) 9   C) 7   D) 0

26. D

27. When folded, 2 is opposite 4, 1 is opposite 5, and 3 is opposite 6. (You can see this by cutting out the diagram shown and folding it into a cube.)

A) 5   B) 3   C) 2   D) 1

27. B

28. Dad took \$205 from his \$300 bank account, leaving \$95. Since the bank deducts \$5 every month he has less than \$100 in that account, it will take 95÷5 = 19 months for the balance to become \$0.

A) 17   B) 18
C) 19   D) 20

28. C

29. 2nd sum: 100 terms, each is a term in 1st sum+100; so 2nd sum = 5050 + 100×100.

A) 10 000   B) 10 050   C) 10 100   D) 15 050

29. D

30. 1243, 1324, 1342, 1423, 1432, 2134, 2143, 2314, 2341, 2413, 2431, 3124, 3142, 3214, 3241, 3412, 3421, 4123, 4132, 4213, 4231, 4312, and 4321.

A) 3   B) 11   C) 17   D) 23

30. D

The end of the contest 🖎 **5**

Visit our Web site at http://www.mathleague.com

6th Grade Solutions

2001-2002 through 2005-2006

Information & Solutions

Tuesday, March 12 or March 19, 2002

Contest Information

6

- **Solutions** Turn the page for detailed contest solutions (written in the question boxes) and letter answers (written in the *Answers* column to the right of each question).

- **Scores** Please remember that *this is a contest, not a test*—and there is no "passing" or "failing" score. Few students score as high as 30 points (75% correct). Students with half that, 15 points, *deserve commendation!*

- **Answers & Rating Scale** Turn to page 148 for the letter answers to each question and the rating scale for this contest.

1. The difference between 34 343 and 1212 is 34 343 − 1212 = 33 131. A) 13 133 B) 22 223 C) 32 222 D) 33 131	1. D
2. (100 − 40) + (90 − 30) + (80 − 20) = 60 + 60 + 60 = 3×60. A) 20 B) 60 C) 80 D) 180	2. B
3. Since 9999, 999, and 99 are all divisible by 9, the remainder is 4. A) 1 B) 3 C) 4 D) 5	3. C
4. 1 million ÷ 500 thousand = 1 000 000 ÷ 500 000 = 10 ÷ 5 = 2. A) 2 B) 10 C) 20 D) 50	4. A
5. $2^4 - 2^3 - 2^2 - 2^1 = 16 - 8 - 4 - 2 = 16 - 14.$ A) 1 B) 2 C) 14 D) 15	5. C
6. Jo is the 12th person "biggied" at McBurgers. *Between* Jo and the 25th person are the 13th, 14th, 15th, . . . , 23rd, and 24th persons. A) 11 B) 12 C) 13 D) 14	6. B
7. The first four odd whole numbers are 1, 3, 5, and 7. Their sum is 16. A) 6 B) 9 C) 10 D) 16	7. D
8. Tens' digit of 22 222×22 222 = tens' digit of (22×22 = 484) = 8. A) 8 B) 6 C) 4 D) 2	8. A
9. 8777 − 7778 = 999 = 444 + 555. A) 445 B) 455 C) 545 D) 555	9. D
10. 12 small balloons weigh 130 kg. Since 72 = 6×12, 72 balloons weigh 6×130 kg = 780 kg. A) 190 kg B) 650 kg C) 780 kg D) 864 kg	10. C
11. 500−350 = 150. Answer = 500+150. A) 200 B) 650 C) 700 D) 850	11. B
12. 400¢÷10¢ = 40, so answer = 40×25¢ = 1000¢ = $10.00 = $10. A) $6 B) $8 C) $10 D) $40	12. C
13. The common factors are 1, 2, 3, 4, 6, and 12 (the factors of 12). A) 4 B) 5 C) 6 D) 8	13. C
14. Use the square of the next prime, and $7^2 = 49$. A) 41 B) 49 C) 67 D) 77	14. B
15. (Average of 16 4s = 4)×(average of 4 16s = 16) = 4×16. A) 4×16 B) 16×16 C) 16×64 D) 64×64	15. A

Go on to the next page ⚫➡ **6**

16. $2002 = 2 \times 7 \times 11 \times 13$, a product of 4 primes > 0. (Note: 1 isn't prime.) A) 2 B) 3 C) 4 D) 5	16. C
17. (3 000 000 birds) ÷ (80 birds per minute) = 37 500 minutes. A) 470 minutes B) 625 minutes C) 2500 minutes D) 37 500 minutes	17. D
18. Rewrite as $(10^3 \times 10^3) + (10^2 \times 10^2) + (10^1 \times 10^1)$. A) $10^6 + 10^4 + 10^2$ B) $2 \times (10^3 + 10^2 + 10^1)$ C) 10^{12} D) $10^9 + 10^4 + 10^1$	18. A
19. A) $.20 \times 80 = 16$ B) $.25 \times 65 = 16.25$ C) $.30 \times 50 = 15$ D) $.35 \times 35 = 12.25$. A) 20% of 80 B) 25% of 65 C) 30% of 50 D) 35% of 35	19. B
20. $1 \times 120 = 2 \times 60 = 3 \times 40 = 4 \times 30 = 5 \times 24 = 6 \times 20 = 8 \times 15 = 10 \times 12$. A) 5 B) 11 C) 15 D) 16	20. D
21. The sum of any 3 whole numbers is always a whole number. A) even B) odd C) prime D) whole	21. D
22. The sum of 5 numbers whose average is 10 is $5 \times 10 = 50$. A) 10 B) 25 C) 50 D) 125	22. C
23. Primes: 2, 3, 5, 7, 11, 13, 17, 19, 23, 29, 31, 37, 41, 43, 47. (1 isn't a prime.) A) 15:25 B) 16:25 C) 15:35 D) 16:34	23. A
24. $\sqrt{16 + 16 + 16 + 16} = \sqrt{4 \times 16}$. A) $\sqrt{4 \times 16}$ B) $4 \times \sqrt{16}$ C) $6 + \sqrt{100}$ D) $\sqrt{100} - \sqrt{36}$	24. A
25. After Sam spent 35% of his money, he had 65%, or \$13, left; 65% : \$13 = 5% : \$1 = 35% : \$7. A) \$6 B) \$7 C) \$20 D) \$23	25. B
26. $3:7 < 7:16$, and both are slightly less than $1:2$, so the answer is B. A) 2 B) 3 C) 4 D) 5	26. B
27. If there's a middle number, it's the average. Its value is $153 \div 9 = 17$. A) 9 B) 13 C) 17 D) 21	27. C
28. Each angle is 90°. The sum is $3 \times 90° = 270°$. A) 120° B) 180° C) 270° D) 360°	28. C
29. Jack was 8 when Jill was 2. He was 10 when she was 4. Now he's 12 and she's 6. The sum of their ages now is $12 + 6 = 18$. A) 8 B) 9 C) 12 D) 18	29. D

Go on to the next page ⟶ **6**

30. $1\times2\times4\times8 = 2^6$; $1\times2\times4\times32 = 2^8$; $1\times2\times4\times512 = 2^{12}$. A) 2^4 B) 2^6 C) 2^8 D) 2^{12}	30. A
31. For bikers A, B, C, D, E, the 10 duets are AB, $AC, AD, AE, BC, BD, BE, CD, CE$, and DE. A) 10 B) 15 C) 20 D) 25	31. A
32. $(2^3\times100^3)\div100^3 = 2^3 = 8 = 200\div25$. A) 100 B) 80 C) 25 D) 8	32. C
33. Every 4th number is divisible by 4, so $\frac{3}{4}\times1000 = 750$ are not. A) 875 B) 850 C) 800 D) 750	33. D
34. The product increases as the numbers get closer, so use $38\times38 = 1444$. A) 5776 B) 5700 C) 1444 D) 1443	34. C
35. If 2 of the 5 consecutive years were leap years, then the total number of days would be $2\times366 + 3\times365 = 1827$. A) 1825 B) 1827 C) 1828 D) 1830	35. B
36. The plane left New York for Vancouver at 2 P.M. and arrived 6 hours later, at 8 P.M. New York time. Vancouver time is 3 hours earlier, so it's 5 P.M. there. A) 11 P.M. B) 9 P.M. C) 8 P.M. D) 5 P.M.	36. D
37. Draw a picture. Area $= \pi r^2$, so a radius of the 1st circle $= 4$ cm, and a radius of 2nd circle $= 2$ cm $=$ the distance between their centers. A) 2 cm B) 4 cm C) 6 cm D) 8 cm	37. A
38. Add 50 to each # on the left. New sum $= 3775 + (50\times50) = 6275$. A) 8775 B) 7550 C) 6275 D) 3825	38. C
39. For fewest "1"s, use 1996 "1"s and 3 "2"s. Their sum is $1996 +2 + 2 + 2 = 2002$. The least number of "1"s that can be used is 1996. A) 1995 B) 1996 C) 1997 D) 1998	39. B
40. A has 4 sides and 2 diagonals. B has 5 sides and 5 diagonals. C has 6 sides and 9 diagonals. D has 8 sides and 20 diagonals. A) square B) pentagon C) hexagon D) octagon	40. B

The end of the contest 🖎 **6**

Visit our Web site at http://www.mathleague.com

Math League Press, P.O. Box 17, Tenafly, New Jersey 07670-0017

Information & Solutions

Tuesday, March 11 or March 18, 2003

Contest Information

- **Solutions** Turn the page for detailed contest solutions (written in the question boxes) and letter answers (written in the *Answers* column to the right of each question).

- **Scores** Please remember that *this is a contest, not a test*—and there is no "passing" or "failing" score. Few students score as high as 30 points (75% correct). Students with half that, 15 points, *deserve commendation!*

- **Answers & Rating Scale** Turn to page 149 for the letter answers to each question and the rating scale for this contest.

1. $20+60 = 80 = 20 \times 4$. A) 2 B) 3 C) 4 D) 6	1. C
2. Two years ago, each was 2 years younger; so the sum was 4 less. A) 24 B) 26 C) 30 D) 32	2. A
3. If I eat 50 drops of ice cream each minute, it will take me 2 minutes to eat 100 drops and 3 minutes for 150 drops. A) $1\frac{1}{2}$ B) 2 C) $2\frac{1}{2}$ D) 3	3. D
4. $(9+1+8+2) \div (7+3+6+4) = 20 \div 20 = 1$. A) 0 B) 1 C) 5 D) 20	4. B
5. Square has 4 sides, triangle 3, and $4-3 = 1$. A) 7 B) 4 C) 3 D) 1	5. D
6. $144 \times 60 = (72 \times 2) \times 60 = 72 \times 120$. A) 72 B) 120 C) 132 D) 140	6. B
7. The gcf of 8 and 4 is 4. The gcf of 8 and 12 is also 4. A) 12 B) 14 C) 16 D) 40	7. A
8. $9 \times 89 = 801 = 899 - 98 = 801$, so choice C is correct. A) 9×98 B) 899×1 C) $899 - 98$ D) $989 - 89$	8. C
9. (# of digits in 1 000 000) : (# of digits in 10 000) = 7:5. A) 2:1 B) 6:5 C) 7:5 D) 5:3	9. C
10. $6400 \div 80 = 80 = 80 \times 1$. A) 1 B) 80 C) 800 D) 6400	10. A
11. Since there are 26 letters in all, 24 come before Y and 1 comes after. A) X B) B C) C D) Y	11. D
12. The day after Tuesday is Wednesday. Three days before Wednesday is Sunday. Mr. Sheep got his diploma on a Sunday. A) Wed. B) Fri. C) Sat. D) Sun.	12. D
13. Every carton holds 12 = 1 dozen eggs; 60 cartons hold 60 dozen. A) 12 dozen B) 60 dozen C) 144 dozen D) 720 dozen	13. B
14. $789 + 98 = (89 + 700) + 98 = 89 + 798$. A) 987 B) 878 C) 798 D) 177	14. C
15. Since 1 is not a prime, the smallest product of primes is $2 \times 3 = 6$. A) 0 B) 3 C) 5 D) 6	15. D
16. $3^2 + 4^2 = 25 = 5^2$. A) 5^2 B) 7^2 C) 12^2 D) 34^2	16. A

Go on to the next page ⅢⅢ➡ **6**

17. Since $0+0 = 0-0 = 0$, their product is $0 \times 0 = 0$. A) 0 B) 1 C) 2 D) 4	17. A
18. Since $90 = 9 \times 10$ and $10-9 = 1$, choice C is correct. A) 63 B) 80 C) 90 D) 99	18. C
19. On vacation, my front teeth hurt on 4 days. My front teeth were OK on 8 days. My vacation lasted $4+8 = 12$ days. A) 2 B) 6 C) 8 D) 12	19. D
20. $4\,km = 4000\,m, 400\,cm = 4\,m; 4004 \div 2 = 2002.$ A) 202 B) 220 C) 2002 D) 22 000	20. C
21. Each of 12 pizzas was cut into 8 slices, for a total of 96 slices. Slices eaten $= 96-4 = 92$. Number of people $= 92 \div 2 = 46$. A) 46 B) 48 C) 92 D) 96	21. A
22. If it were a square, its dimensions would be 6×6. But it's not. A) 4 B) 6 C) 9 D) 12	22. B
23. 28 and 32 are divisible by 1, 2, and 4, the 3 common factors. A) 2 B) 3 C) 4 D) 5	23. B
24. $12 \div 6 = 2$; $12 \div 4 = 3$; 12 is the LCM of 4 and 6. A) 2 B) 6 C) 12 D) 24	24. C
25. Only choice B results in a prime after 1 is subtracted: $48-1 = 47$, which is a prime. A) 46 B) 48 C) 50 D) 53	25. B
26. $225¢ \div 15¢ = 15$, and $150¢ \div 15¢ = 10$, so Di can buy $15-10 = 5$ more than Al. A) 5 B) 10 C) 15 D) 25	26. A
27. Add first, then round: $3.83+2.34 = 6.17$. Round up to 6.2. A) 6.1 B) 6.17 C) 6.18 D) 6.2	27. D
28. It's now 12:31 P.M., so 31 minutes later is 1:02 P.M. A) 12:31 A.M. B) 1:02 A.M. C) 12:31 P.M. D) 1:02 P.M.	28. D
29. If the larger of two consecutive whole numbers has one more digit than the smaller, their ones' digits must be 9 and 0. A) 10 B) 9 C) 1 D) 0	29. B

Go on to the next page ⟱ **6**

30. Dave ran 2 km at 8 km/hr., so it took him (60÷4) min. Andy ran 2 km at 10 km/hr., so it took him (60÷5) min. Diff. is 15−12 = 3. A) 2 B) 3 C) 12 D) 15	30. B
31. (My current age − 10) + (my current age + 10) = 2×(my current age), so A is the answer. A) 2 B) 3 C) 4 D) 10	31. A
32. Every 4 seasons, it's winter. Since 2003 = (4×500)+3, Dino becomes an adult 3 seasons after winter, in autumn. A) spring B) summer C) autumn D) winter	32. C
33. 35 sips = 10 slurps; 10 slurps = 4 gulps; so 35 sips = 4 gulps. A) 3 gulps B) 4 gulps C) 5 gulps D) 7 gulps	33. B
34. The width of a 3×6 rectangle is half the length, and the area is 18. A square with the same width would have an area of $3^2 = 9$. A) 6 B) 9 C) 27 D) 36	34. B
35. My address is a 2-digit number. The product and sum of the digits are equal. Since 2+2 = 4 = 2×2, my address is 22. A) 10 B) 11 C) 21 D) 22	35. D
36. It takes me (52×2) weeks = 104 weeks to read 52 books. A) 26 weeks B) 52 weeks C) 54 weeks D) 104 weeks	36. D
37. All such numbers must be odd, but need not be prime; try 143 = 11×13. A) even B) prime C) odd D) negative	37. C
38. The minute hand goes once around the face of a circular clock each hour. To go around 60 times would take 60 hours. A) 1 B) 60 C) 360 D) 3600	38. B
39. From 100 to 999, there are 999−100+1 = 900 3-digit numbers. A) 1000 B) 999 C) 900 D) 899	39. C
40. Since $2^2 + 3^2 + 4^2 = 4 + 9 + 16 = 29$, the sides of the squares are 2, 3, and 4. A side of the largest square is 4. A) 4 B) 5 C) 9 D) 16	40. A

The end of the contest ✍ **6**

Visit our Web site at http://www.mathleague.com

SIXTH GRADE MATHEMATICS CONTEST

Math League Press, P.O. Box 17, Tenafly, New Jersey 07670-0017

Information & Solutions

Tuesday, March 9 or 16, 2004

Contest Information

6

- **Solutions** Turn the page for detailed contest solutions (written in the question boxes) and letter answers (written in the *Answers* column to the right of each question).

- **Scores** Please remember that *this is a contest, not a test*—and there is no "passing" or "failing" score. Few students score as high as 30 points (75% correct). Students with half that, 15 points, *deserve commendation!*

- **Answers & Rating Scale** Turn to page 150 for the letter answers to each question and the rating scale for this contest.

1.	When an odd number is divided by 2, the remainder is 1. A) 0 B) 1 C) 2 D) prime	1. B
2.	For every two men who prefer stripes, one prefers solids. So, 40 prefer stripes and 20 prefer solids. A) 15 B) 20 C) 30 D) 40	2. D
3.	Since $4 = 2^2$, choice D is correct. A) 4444 B) 444 C) 44 D) 4	3. D
4.	$88 \times 44 = 11 \times 8 \times 11 \times 4 = 11 \times 11 \times 32$. A) 12 B) 20 C) 32 D) 122	4. C
5.	Work backwards: $37 - 9 = 28$, and $28 \div 2 = 14$. A) 14 B) 15 C) 19 D) 28	5. A
6.	Subtracting $(10+20+30+40)$ leaves $(100+100+100+100) = 400$. A) 270 B) 310 C) 330 D) 400	6. D
7.	$2^2 + 2^2 + 2^2 + 2^2 = 4 + 4 + 4 + 4 = 16 = 4^2$. A) 4^2 B) 8^2 C) 16^2 D) 22^2	7. A
8.	Since $7 \times 7 + 7 \times 7 = 49 + 49 = 98 = 14 \times 7$, choice A is correct. A) 14 B) 21 C) 49 D) 56	8. A
9.	(# of digits in $1\,000\,000$) : (# of digits in $12\,000\,000$) = 7:8. A) 1:12 B) 1:2 C) 3:4 D) 7:8	9. D
10.	$111 + 999 = 1110 = 5 \times 222$. A) 110 B) 111 C) 220 D) 222	10. D
11.	Area of a square = $\text{side}^2 = 6^2 = 36$. Perimeter = $4 \times \text{side} = 24$. Subtracting, $36 - 24 = 12$. A) 6 B) 12 C) 18 D) 24	11. B
12.	At my fastest, I carve 40 letters a day. At that rate, I'll need $(180 \div 40) = 4\frac{1}{2}$ days to carve 180 letters. A) 4 B) $4\frac{1}{2}$ C) 5 D) $5\frac{1}{2}$	12. B
13.	$11 \times 100 = 1100 = 110 \times 10 = 111 \times 10 - 10$. A) 0 B) 1 C) 10 D) 11	13. C
14.	25% of 1 hour = 25% of 60 mins. = 1/4 of 60 mins. = 15 mins. A) 10 B) 12 C) 15 D) 25	14. C
15.	$9 \times 9 \div 3 = 81 \div 3 = 27 = 3 \times 9$. A) 1 B) 3 C) 3^2 D) 3^3	15. C
16.	(989 rounded to the nearest ten) $-$ (989) = $990 - 989 = 1$. A) 0 B) 1 C) 3 D) 10	16. B

17. Think of the shape of a sugar cube: it has 6 faces. A) 2 　　　 B) 3 　　　 C) 4 　　　 D) 6	17. D
18. Since 2004 = 4×501, its largest odd divisor is 501. A) 3 　　　 B) 167 　　　 C) 501 　　　 D) 1001	18. C
19. The sum of the 3 angles of a triangle is 180°, and $180° \div 3 = 60°$. A) 30° 　　　 B) 45° 　　　 C) 60° 　　　 D) 90°	19. C
20. Half my number is 6, so my number is 12. Its square is $12^2 = 144$. A) 9 　　 B) 36 　　 C) 81 　　 D) 144	20. D
21. A triangle with integer sides has perimeter 6. Each of the 3 sides *must* have length 2. A) 3 　　　　 B) 2 C) 1 　　　　 D) 0	21. A
22. $3 \times 4 \times 25¢ = 300¢ = 5 \times 6 \times 10¢$. A) dimes 　　 B) dollars 　　 C) nickels 　　 D) pennies	22. A
23. The divisors of 9 are 1, 3, and 9. All the others have 4 divisors. A) 6 　　　 B) 8 　　　 C) 9 　　　 D) 10	23. C
24. $\sqrt{4^2 + 4^2 + 4^2 + 4^2} = \sqrt{16 + 16 + 16 + 16} = \sqrt{64} = 8 = 2 \times 4$. A) 4 　　　 B) 8 　　　 C) 4^2 　　　 D) 8^2	24. A
25. The 8 such primes are 11, 13, 17, 19, 23, 29, 31, and 37. A) 7 　　　 B) 8 　　　 C) 13 　　　 D) 14	25. B
26. If I have 21 hands, I may have 10 that point right, 10 that don't point at all, and only 1 that points left. But if I have 22 hands, at least 2 must point left. A) 6 　 B) 11 　 C) 21 　 D) 22	26. D
27. If the average is 10, the numbers must be 8, 9, 10, 11, and 12. A) 10 　 B) 12 　 C) 13 　 D) 15	27. B
28. One of each coin totals 41¢, so I must have a multiple of 41¢. I could have $1 \times 41¢ = 41¢$, or $3 \times 41¢ = \$1.23$, or $6 \times 41¢ = \$2.46$. A) 41¢ 　　 B) \$1.23 　　 C) \$1.68 　　 D) \$2.46	28. C
29. Use ratios: $30\% : 60 = 70\% : ?$. Now, $? = 2 \times 70 = 140$. A) 70 　　　 B) 100 　　　 C) 130 　　　 D) 140	29. D
30. Since 10 is half my age, I'm 20 now; 4 years ago I was 16. A) 20 　　　 B) 16 　　　 C) 14 　　　 D) 6	30. B

31. Area of one square $= 144 \div 4 = 36$, so each square's side $= 6$. Distance around shaded region $= 8$ sides $= 8 \times 6 = 48$.

    A) 36   B) 48   C) 60   D) 108

    31. B

32. $1 \times 2 \times 3 \times 4 \times 5 = 120$, so $120\,000 = 1 \times 2 \times 3 \times 4 \times 5 \times 1000$, and the greatest possible value of one of the six integers is 1000.

    A) 1000   B) 2000   C) 3000   D) 6000

    32. A

33. If every gumball weighs 3 g, then a machine that holds 3000 g of gumballs holds 1000 gumballs.

    A) 100   B) 300   C) 1000   D) 3000

    33. C

34. Ten such #s are 101,111,...,191. With 9 choices for 1st & last digits, there are $10 \times 9 = 90$ such numbers.

    A) 81   B) 90   C) 99   D) 100

    34. B

35. The sum of 500 odd numbers is even. Now we add only even numbers, so the final sum is even.

    A) even   B) odd   C) prime   D) negative

    35. A

36. Each triangle uses 3 dots, so each *does not* use 1 dot. There are 4 ways to *not* use 1 of the 4 dots, hence 4 triangles.

    A) 2   B) 3   C) 4   D) 5

    36. C

37. The four largest possible missing digits are 9, 8, 6, and 5. The sum of all 6 digits is $1+7+9+8+6+5 = 36$. The largest possible average of all 6 digits is $36 \div 6 = 6$.

    A) 4   B) 6   C) $6\frac{1}{2}$ D) 7

    37. B

38. Coach ran the 1st half twice as fast as he ran the 2nd half, so it took him 10 mins. to run the 1st 2 km. and 20 mins. to run the last 2 km. A speed of 2 km in 20 mins. is the same as a speed of 6 km in 60 mins., or 6 km/hr.

    A) 4   B) 6   C) 8   D) 12

    38. B

39. $6 \times 35 = 2 \times 3 \times 5 \times 7$, so choice D has the most prime factors, four.

    A) 1×121 B) 11×15
    C) 7×19 D) 6×35

    39. D

40. If the 1st is a Saturday, so are the 8th, 15th, 22nd, & 29th. The 30th is a Sunday, which gives us 5 Saturdays and 5 Sundays.

    A) Thursday   B) Friday   C) Saturday   D) Sunday

    40. C

The end of the contest **6**

Visit our Web site at http://www.mathleague.com

Information & Solutions

Tuesday, March 8, 2005

Contest Information

- **Solutions** Turn the page for detailed contest solutions (written in the question boxes) and letter answers (written in the *Answers* column to the right of each question).

- **Scores** Please remember that *this is a contest, not a test*—and there is no "passing" or "failing" score. Few students score as high as 30 points (75% correct). Students with half that, 15 points, *deserve commendation!*

- **Answers & Rating Scale** Turn to page 151 for the letter answers to each question and the rating scale for this contest.

1. Since $\frac{1}{2} = 0.5$, $\frac{3}{4} = 0.75$, & $0.5 < 0.6 < 0.75$, choice C is correct. A) 0.2　　　　B) 0.4　　　　C) 0.6　　　　D) 0.8	1. C
2. A polygon must have 3 or more sides. A) 2　　B) 3　　C) 4　　D) 21	2. A
3. Since 5 weeks = (5×7) days = 35 days, I must have watched my mail for 35 days − 5 days = 30 days. A) 10　　B) 25　　C) 30　　D) 35	3. C
4. $1010 + 10\,100 = 11\,110 = 10 \times 1111$. A) 101　　B) 1010　　C) 1020　　D) 1111	4. D
5. $500¢ \div 10¢ = 50$ and $1000¢ \div 25¢ = 40$, and 50-40 = 10. A) 0　　　　B) 2　　　　C) 5　　　　D) 10	5. D
6. Since 10% of # = 100, $10 \times (10\%$ of #$) = 10 \times 100 = 1000$. A) 10　　　　B) 100　　　　C) 110　　　　D) 1000	6. D
7. $(12+10+8+6+4+2) \div (6+5+4+3+2+1) = 42 \div 21 = 2$. A) 60　　　　B) 45　　　　C) 6　　　　D) 2	7. D
8. Divide each answer choice by 2, then check for a multiple of 6. A) 28　　　　B) 30　　　　C) 36　　　　D) 42	8. C
9. $54 \div 3 = 18 = 3 \times 6$.　　A) 6　B) 18　C) 54　D) 162	9. A
10. The area of the wall is $4 \times 4 = 16$. Since the roll covers half the wall, the area of the part covered by this roll is 8. A) 4　　　　B) 8　　　　C) 16　　　　D) 32	10. B
11. I need 12 pieces of fruit to make 3 glasses of juice, so I need 4 pieces to make 1 glass. I need $4 \times 10 = 40$ pieces for 10 glasses. A) 30　　B) 36　　C) 40　　D) 120	11. C
12. The only positive divisor of 100 that is a multiple of 100 is 100. A) 1　　B) 10　　C) 25　　D) 100	12. A
13. A *hendecagon* is an 11-sided polygon. The product of the number of sides of a hendecagon and of a square is $11 \times 4 = 44$. A) 44　　　　B) 55　　　　C) 66　　　　D) 88	13. A
14. (number of 0s in 1000):(number of 0s in 1 000 000) = 3:6 = 1:2. A) 1:1　　　　B) 1:2　　　　C) 2:3　　　　D) 4:7	14. B
15. Every even number has a factor of 2, and 2 is an even prime. A) even　　　　B) odd　　　　C) prime　　　　D) whole	15. A

Go on to the next page ⟫ **6**

16. In 1 second, your rocket flies 300 m = 300×100 cm = 30 000 cm and my pet runs 300 cm. Speed ratio = 30 000:300 = 100:1 = 100. A) 30 000 B) 10 000 C) 300 D) 100	16. D
17. As shown below, the sum can be any of the choices *except* C. A) 12 = 4+8 B) 18 = 2+16 C) 32 D) 33 = 1+32	17. C
18. The avg. of any odd # of *consecutive* integers is the middle one. A) 15 B) 16 C) 19 D) 135	18. A
19. Since each act has 4 scenes, there are 3×4 = 12 scenes in all. The total number of characters in the play is 2×12 = 24. A) 6 B) 8 C) 12 D) 24	19. D
20. If 3/4 are bills, then 1/4 are not. The ratio of the # of bills to the # of other letters is (3/4):(1/4) = 3:1. **We Get Letters..** A) 7:1 B) 7:3 C) 3:1 D) 3:4	20. C
21. $4 \times 4^4 = 4^1 \times 4^4 = 4^{1+4} = 4^5$. A) 4^4 B) 4^5 C) 14^4 D) 16^5	21. B
22. For choices B, C, D, (# pennies, # nickels, # dimes) is shown. A) 11¢ B) 19¢ (9,0,1) C) 30¢ (5,5,0) D) 31¢ (6,3,1)	22. A
23. Of the choices listed, only 900 is the square of an integer. A) 600 B) 700 C) 800 D) 900	23. D
24. 75 nickels = 375¢ = (375÷25) quarters = 15 quarters. A) 3 B) 15 C) 25 D) 375	24. B
25. There is no factor of 7 in 30×40×50, so choice C is correct. A) 1×3×5 B) 2×4×6 C) 5×7×9 D) 6×8×10	25. C
26. Ten years ago, Ted's age was (22÷2) = 11. His age today is 11+10 = 21. A) 16 B) 21 C) 32 D) 42	26. B
27. If all tents hold 2, we can hold only 12. But if 3 hold 2 and 3 hold 4, we can hold (3×2)+(3×4) = 18 campers. A) 4 B) 3 C) 2 D) 1	27. B
28. If 3 out of 5 dentists recommend sugarless gum, then 2 out of 5 = 20 out of 50 = 40 out of 100 = 40% *don't*. A) 20% B) 30% C) 40% D) 60%	28. C
29. 6 mins. after noon is 12:06 P.M.; 6 hrs. before that is 6:06 A.M. A) 6:06 A.M. B) 6:06 P.M. C) 5:54 A.M. D) 5:54 P.M.	29. A

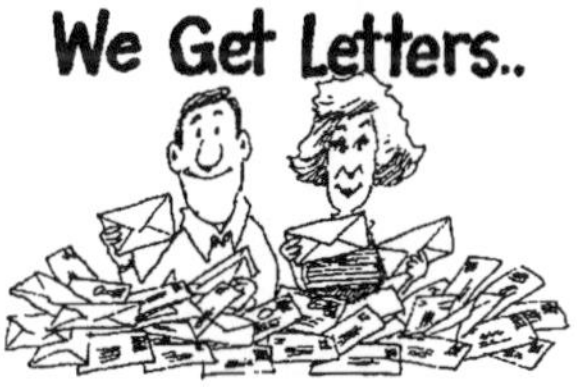

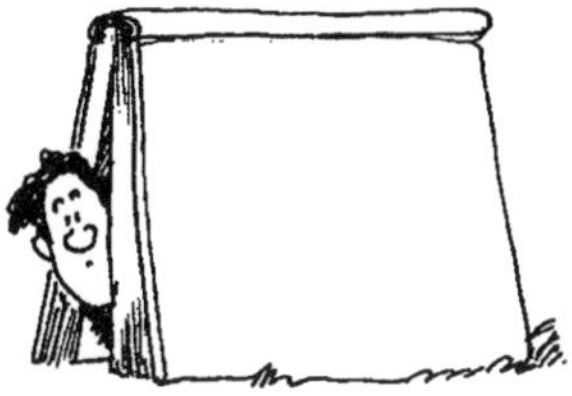

Go on to the next page ⫸ **6**

30.	There are 90 2-digit numbers starting with 10 and ending with 99. Exactly half of them have an even digit-sum. A) 45 B) 48 C) 50 D) 52	30. A
31.	80 km in 60 min. = 8 km in 6 min. = 24 km in 18 min. A) 20 B) 24 C) 28 D) 30	31. B
32.	$2^{2005} = 2^1 \times 2^{2004} = 2^{2004} + 2^{2004}$. A) 1 B) 2 C) 2004 D) 2^{2004}	32. D
33.	The sum is 2+3+5+7+(1+1)+(1+3)+(1+7)+(1+9) = 41. A) 77 B) 76 C) 41 D) 40	33. C
34.	If 4 pears weigh as much as 6 peaches, and 6 peaches weigh as much as 90 grapes, then 4 pears weigh as much as 90 grapes. A) 4 B) 6 C) 8 D) 12	34. A
35.	The perimeter of the square is 32. A side has length 8, and the area is 64. Half of the square is shaded, so the shaded area is 32. A) 4 B) 8 C) 16 D) 32	35. D
36.	$(51 - 1) + (52 - 2) + \ldots + (99 - 49) + (100 - 50) = 50 + 50 + \ldots + 50 + 50 = 50 \times 50 = 2500$. A) 2000 B) 2500 C) 2550 D) 5000	36. B
37.	I spent $360 for 110 services, 100 with a smile, 10 without. The 10 without a smile cost as much as 20 with a smile. It costs $360 for 120 services with a smile, or $3 for one service with a smile. A) $3.00 B) $3.15 C) $3.30 D) $3.45	37. A
38.	In 24 hours, the hour hand goes around the clock 2 times, the minute hand 24 times, and the second hand $60 \times 24 = 1440$ times. A) 144 B) 1440 C) 1466 D) 86 400	38. C
39.	Try $2 \times 3 \times 5 = 60$, which is divisible by 2×3, 2×5, 3×5, & $2 \times 3 \times 5$. The product of 3 primes is *always* divisible by 4 non-primes > 1. A) 1 B) 2 C) 3 D) 4	39. D
40.	Keep adding consecutive integers until you reach 120¢: 1¢ + 2¢ + 3¢ + ... + 14¢ + 15¢ = 120¢, so I am 15 years old. A) 10 B) 12 C) 15 D) 20	40. C

The end of the contest **6**

SIXTH GRADE MATHEMATICS CONTEST

Math League Press, P.O. Box 17, Tenafly, New Jersey 07670-0017

Information & Solutions

Tuesday, February 28, 2006

Contest Information

6

- **Solutions** Turn the page for detailed contest solutions (written in the question boxes) and letter answers (written in the *Answers* column to the right of each question).

- **Scores** Please remember that *this is a contest, not a test*—and there is no "passing" or "failing" score. Few students score as high as 30 points (75% correct). Students with half that, 15 points, *deserve commendation!*

- **Answers & Rating Scale** Turn to page 152 for the letter answers to each question and the rating scale for this contest.

133

1. $(75+25) + (76+24) = 100 + 100 = 200.$
   A) 200 B) 201 C) 202 D) 203

   1. A

2. 3 pies require 2 dozen apples = 24 apples, so 6 pies require 48.
   A) 12 B) 18 C) 36 D) 48

   2. D

3. $8\times9 = 9\times8 = 9\times2\times4 = 18\times4.$
   A) threes B) fours C) nines D) nineteens

   3. B

4. If 2 of every 3 such bears wear red tutus, then $2\times8 = 16$ of every (3×8) bears wear red tutus.
   A) 8 B) 12 C) 16 D) 18

   4. C

5. $20\times30\times40 = (20\times\mathbf{3})\times(\mathbf{10}\times40) = 60\times400.$
   A) 300 B) 400 C) 500 D) 1200

   5. B

6. Since $55\times55 = 3025$, the tens' digit is 2.
   A) 7 B) 5 C) 3 D) 2

   6. D

7. The sum of the measures of all the angles in any triangle is 180°.
   A) 360° B) 270° C) 180° D) 90°

   7. C

8. June is 3 months after March. It's also 4 months before October.
   A) 1 B) 2 C) 3 D) 4

   8. D

9. When 305 is divided by 25, the remainder is 5. Since 3005 is a multiple of 5, the remainder when 3005 is divided by 5 is 0.
   A) 0 B) 5 C) 95 D) 160

   9. A

10. $2\div1 = 2$, and $22+44 = 66$. The answer to $66\div\underline{\ ?\ } = 2$ is 33.
    A) $(2+4)$ B) 11 C) 22 D) $(11+22)$

    10. D

11. The area of a circle is twice the area of its semi-circle.
    A) 4 B) 1/4 C) 1/2 D) 2

    11. D

12. There is only 1 even prime number, 2.
    A) 0 B) 1 C) 2 D) 3

    12. B

13. Our town's mayor gives speeches all the time. So far this year, he's made $2+2^2+5+5^2 = 2+4+5+25 = 36 = 6^2$ speeches.
    A) $7+7^2$ B) 6^2 C) 10^2 D) 14^2

    13. B

14. $1800\div30 = 60 = 30\times2.$
    A) 2 B) 6 C) 54 D) 60

    14. A

15. Perimeter of a rectangle $= 2\times(\text{length} + \text{width}) = \text{even }\#.$
    A) even B) odd C) 4 D) prime

    15. A

Go on to the next page ⏵ **6**

| 16. | *Eight hundred thousand fifty* = 800 050 has 4 0s. | 16. B |
| | A) 3 B) 4 C) 5 D) 6 | |

| 17. | I can mail 600 000 cards in $600\,000 \div 3000 = 200$ days. | 17. B |
| | A) 100 B) 200 C) 1000 D) 2000 | |

| 18. | A pentagon has 5 sides, so the average side-length is $60 \div 5 = 12$. | 18. C |
| | A) 6 B) 10 C) 12 D) 15 | |

19. Giant sandwiches come prepackaged. I can buy 1 for $30, 3 for $75, or 5 for $100. I can buy (4×5) for $(4 \times \$100)$. I can buy 20 giant sandwiches for $400. [NOTE: This will leave $25 unspent.]

A) 18   B) 19   C) 20   D) 21

19. C

| 20. | The factors of 48 are 1, **2**, 3, **4, 6, 8, 12, 16, 24**, and **48**. | 20. C |
| | A) 5 B) 7 C) 8 D) 9 | |

| 21. | The product of the first 3 or more primes has $2 \times 5 = 10$ as a factor. | 21. A |
| | A) 0 B) 2 C) 4 D) 6 | |

| 22. | In a *scalene* triangle all three sides have different lengths. | 22. D |
| | A) rhombus B) rectangle C) square D) triangle | |

| 23. | The gcf of $2 \times 3 \times 4 \times 5$ and $2 \times 3 \times 7 \times 4 \times 2 \times 9$ is $2 \times 3 \times 4 = 24$. | 23. C |
| | A) 6 B) 8 C) 24 D) 48 | |

| 24. | My allowance is now $2. Last year, it was $1. Two years ago, it was 50¢. Three years ago, my allowance was 25¢. | 24. A |
| | A) 25¢ B) 50¢ C) 70¢ D) 75¢ | |

| 25. | 1111 mins. = 18 hrs. 31 mins, so it's 5:42 A.M. | 25. C |
| | A) 5:11 A.M. B) 5:40 A.M. C) 5:42 A.M. D) 6:01 A.M. | |

| 26. | Since we won every odd-numbered game, we won our 87th, 89th, 91st, . . . , and 101st games. That's 8 of our last 15. | 26. B |
| | A) 7 B) 8 C) 12 D) 13 | |

27. (0.75×12) slices = 9 slices.

A) 7   B) 8   C) 9   D) 10

27. C

28. $9 + 16 + 144 = 169 = 13^2$.

A) 13^2 B) 15^2 C) 17^2 D) 19^2

28. A

| 29. | Since 5 years = 60 months and $5 + 60 = 65$, I am now 5 years old. In 5 years, I will be 10. | 29. B |
| | A) 9 B) 10 C) 11 D) 12 | |

30. 3 cartoons last at least $3 \times 5 = 15$ mins. and at most $3 \times 8 = 24$ mins. They could *not* last more than 24 mins. A) 15 B) 18 C) 24 D) 25	30. D
31. It takes 12 hours for the hour hand to complete its first revolution, which begins at midnight and ends at noon. A) 1 A.M. B) 1 P.M. C) midnight D) noon	31. D
32. The average weight of all 5 sacks is $40 \text{ kg} \div 5 = 8 \text{ kg} = 2$ blue sacks. So, 1 blue sack = 4 kg. The average weight of 1 red sack is $(40 \text{ kg} - 4 \text{ kg}) \div 4 = 9 \text{ kg}$. A) 36 B) 9 C) 8 D) 4	32. B
33. Side of square = 6 = circle's diam.; circle's area = $\pi r^2 = 3^2 \pi = 9\pi$. A) 3π B) 6π C) 9π D) 36π	33. C
34. The only factor common to 2 different primes is 1, an odd number. A) odd B) even C) prime D) 0	34. A
35. 15 hip-hops = (3×5) hip-hops = (2×3) hops = (2×1) hips, so 15 hip-hops = 2 hips. A) 2 B) 3 C) 5 D) 6	35. A
36. I sell 3 tickets every 10 minutes = 9 every 30 minutes. You sell 4 tickets every 12 minutes = 1 every 3 minutes = 10 every 30 minutes. We sell a total 19 tickets every 30 minutes. A) 7, 9 B) 11, 15 C) 12, 20 D) 19, 30	36. D
37. If I multiply a whole number by 5, the product is divisible by 5. If I add 1 to this product, the result is *no longer* divisible by 5. A) 2 B) 3 C) 4 D) 5	37. D
38. The square is divided into 8 identical triangles. Each triangle has area $144 \div 8 = 18$. The area of the shaded region is the area of 2 triangles or $2 \times 18 = 36$. A) 72 B) 36 C) 18 D) 12	38. B
39. Each of the next 10 consec. integers is 10 more than one of the 1st ten. The sum of the larger numbers is $5005 + (10 \times 10) = 5105$. A) 5015 B) 5050 C) 5105 D) 50 105	39. C
40. 180 000 000 secs. = $(180\,000\,000 \div 60)$ mins. = $(3\,000\,000 \div 60)$ hrs. A) 5 000 000 B) 50 000 C) 5000 D) 50	40. B

The end of the contest ✍ **6**

Visit our Web site at http://www.mathleague.com

Answer Keys & Difficulty Ratings

• • • • • • • • • • • • • • • • • •

2001-2002 through 2005-2006

ANSWERS, 2001-02 4th Grade Contest

1. A	7. C	13. A	19. D	25. A
2. D	8. B	14. C	20. B	26. B
3. D	9. C	15. C	21. A	27. D
4. A	10. B	16. D	22. B	28. C
5. B	11. D	17. B	23. B	29. C
6. C	12. D	18. C	24. A	30. A

RATE YOURSELF!!!
for the 2001-02 4th GRADE CONTEST

Score	Rating
28-30	Another Einstein
26-27	Mathematical Wizard
23-25	School Champion
19-22	Grade Level Champion
17-18	Best In The Class
15-16	Excellent Student
11-14	Good Student
9-10	Average Student
0-8	Better Luck Next Time

ANSWERS, 2002-03 4th Grade Contest

1. A	7. A	13. B	19. D	25. B
2. A	8. D	14. C	20. B	26. C
3. D	9. D	15. D	21. C	27. D
4. C	10. D	16. A	22. A	28. B
5. D	11. B	17. C	23. D	29. B
6. A	12. D	18. A	24. C	30. A

RATE YOURSELF!!!
for the 2002-03 4th GRADE CONTEST

Score	Rating
28-30	Another Einstein
25-27	Mathematical Wizard
23-24	School Champion
20-22	Grade Level Champion
17-19	Best In The Class
14-16	Excellent Student
12-13	Good Student
10-11	Average Student
0-9	Better Luck Next Time

ANSWERS, 2003-04 4th Grade Contest

1. C	7. B	13. C	19. C	25. C
2. D	8. D	14. C	20. A	26. B
3. C	9. B	15. A	21. B	27. D
4. A	10. D	16. D	22. B	28. A
5. C	11. A	17. D	23. C	29. A
6. B	12. A	18. D	24. B	30. D

RATE YOURSELF!!!
for the 2003-04 4th GRADE CONTEST

Score	Rating
28-30	Another Einstein
25-27	Mathematical Wizard
22-24	School Champion
20-21	Grade Level Champion
18-19	Best In The Class
15-17	Excellent Student
12-14	Good Student
9-11	Average Student
0-8	Better Luck Next Time

ANSWERS, 2004-05 4th Grade Contest

1. C	7. D	13. B	19. C	25. D
2. A	8. B	14. A	20. D	26. A
3. C	9. D	15. C	21. C	27. B
4. B	10. B	16. D	22. C	28. B
5. A	11. C	17. A	23. C	29. A
6. A	12. B	18. B	24. A	30. D

RATE YOURSELF!!!
for the 2004-05 4th GRADE CONTEST

Score	Rating
29-30	Another Einstein
27-28	Mathematical Wizard
24-26	School Champion
22-23	Grade Level Champion
19-21	Best In The Class
16-18	Excellent Student
13-15	Good Student
11-12	Average Student
0-10	Better Luck Next Time

ANSWERS, 2005-06 4th Grade Contest

1. C	7. C	13. B	19. A	25. C
2. A	8. B	14. C	20. A	26. C
3. B	9. D	15. A	21. B	27. D
4. D	10. C	16. D	22. B	28. B
5. A	11. B	17. B	23. C	29. D
6. D	12. A	18. D	24. A	30. B

RATE YOURSELF!!!
for the 2005-06 4th GRADE CONTEST

Score	Rating
29-30	Another Einstein
26-28	Mathematical Wizard
24-25	School Champion
22-23	Grade Level Champion
19-21	Best In The Class
17-18	Excellent Student
14-16	Good Student
11-13	Average Student
0-10	Better Luck Next Time

ANSWERS, 2001-02 5th Grade Contest

1. D	7. C	13. B	19. B	25. C
2. D	8. D	14. A	20. A	26. D
3. B	9. C	15. D	21. D	27. A
4. A	10. C	16. B	22. D	28. C
5. C	11. B	17. C	23. D	29. A
6. A	12. B	18. C	24. B	30. B

RATE YOURSELF!!!
for the 2001-02 5th GRADE CONTEST

Score	Rating
28-30	Another Einstein
26-27	Mathematical Wizard
24-25	School Champion
22-23	Grade Level Champion
19-21	Best In The Class
17-18	Excellent Student
14-16	Good Student
11-13	Average Student
0-10	Better Luck Next Time

ANSWERS, 2002-03 5th Grade Contest

1. D	7. A	13. D	19. D	25. A
2. B	8. C	14. C	20. B	26. A
3. C	9. A	15. D	21. B	27. B
4. D	10. D	16. A	22. D	28. A
5. D	11. B	17. A	23. C	29. D
6. B	12. C	18. B	24. D	30. C

RATE YOURSELF!!!
for the 2002-03 5th GRADE CONTEST

Score	Rating
28-30	Another Einstein
26-27	Mathematical Wizard
23-25	School Champion
21-22	Grade Level Champion
18-20	Best In The Class
15-17	Excellent Student
13-14	Good Student
10-12	Average Student
0-9	Better Luck Next Time

ANSWERS, 2003-04 5th Grade Contest

1. A	7. B	13. D	19. C	25. A
2. C	8. A	14. D	20. B	26. C
3. C	9. D	15. B	21. D	27. D
4. B	10. C	16. C	22. A	28. C
5. A	11. B	17. A	23. B	29. D
6. D	12. C	18. D	24. B	30. D

RATE YOURSELF!!!
for the 2003-04 5th GRADE CONTEST

Score	Rating
29-30	Another Einstein
26-28	Mathematical Wizard
23-25	School Champion
20-22	Grade Level Champion
17-19	Best In The Class
14-16	Excellent Student
12-13	Good Student
9-11	Average Student
0-8	Better Luck Next Time

ANSWERS, 2004-05 5th Grade Contest

1. C	7. D	13. B	19. C	25. C
2. D	8. A	14. C	20. D	26. D
3. A	9. C	15. C	21. B	27. B
4. D	10. A	16. D	22. A	28. B
5. C	11. B	17. C	23. A	29. D
6. B	12. B	18. C	24. A	30. C

RATE YOURSELF!!!
for the 2004-05 5th GRADE CONTEST

Score	Rating
28-30	Another Einstein
26-27	Mathematical Wizard
24-25	School Champion
22-23	Grade Level Champion
19-21	Best In The Class
16-18	Excellent Student
13-15	Good Student
11-12	Average Student
0-10	Better Luck Next Time

ANSWERS, 2005-06 5th Grade Contest

1. B	7. B	13. D	19. B	25. B
2. B	8. D	14. C	20. A	26. D
3. C	9. A	15. B	21. B	27. B
4. D	10. A	16. A	22. A	28. C
5. A	11. D	17. D	23. A	29. D
6. C	12. B	18. D	24. C	30. D

RATE YOURSELF!!!
for the 2005-06 5th GRADE CONTEST

Score	Rating
28-30	Another Einstein
26-27	Mathematical Wizard
24-25	School Champion
22-23	Grade Level Champion
19-21	Best In The Class
17-18	Excellent Student
14-16	Good Student
12-13	Average Student
0-11	Better Luck Next Time

ANSWERS, 2001-02 6th Grade Contest

1. D	9. D	17. D	25. B	33. D
2. B	10. C	18. A	26. B	34. C
3. C	11. B	19. B	27. C	35. B
4. A	12. C	20. D	28. C	36. D
5. C	13. C	21. D	29. D	37. A
6. B	14. B	22. C	30. A	38. C
7. D	15. A	23. A	31. A	39. B
8. A	16. C	24. A	32. C	40. B

RATE YOURSELF!!!
for the 2001-02 6th GRADE CONTEST

Score	Rating
36-40	Another Einstein
33-35	Mathematical Wizard
30-32	School Champion
26-29	Grade Level Champion
23-25	Best In The Class
19-22	Excellent Student
16-18	Good Student
13-15	Average Student
0-12	Better Luck Next Time

ANSWERS, 2002-03 6th Grade Contest

1. C	9. C	17. A	25. B	33. B
2. A	10. A	18. C	26. A	34. B
3. D	11. D	19. D	27. D	35. D
4. B	12. D	20. C	28. D	36. D
5. D	13. B	21. A	29. B	37. C
6. B	14. C	22. B	30. B	38. B
7. A	15. D	23. B	31. A	39. C
8. C	16. A	24. C	32. C	40. A

RATE YOURSELF!!!
for the 2002-03 6th GRADE CONTEST

Score	Rating
39-40	Another Einstein
36-38	Mathematical Wizard
33-35	School Champion
29-32	Grade Level Champion
26-28	Best In The Class
23-25	Excellent Student
19-22	Good Student
15-18	Average Student
0-14	Better Luck Next Time

ANSWERS, 2003-04 6th Grade Contest

1. B	9. D	17. D	25. B	33. C
2. D	10. D	18. C	26. D	34. B
3. D	11. B	19. C	27. B	35. A
4. C	12. B	20. D	28. C	36. C
5. A	13. C	21. A	29. D	37. B
6. D	14. C	22. A	30. B	38. B
7. A	15. C	23. C	31. B	39. D
8. A	16. B	24. A	32. A	40. C

RATE YOURSELF!!!
for the 2003-04 6th GRADE CONTEST

Score	Rating
38-40	Another Einstein
35-37	Mathematical Wizard
32-34	School Champion
29-31	Grade Level Champion
26-28	Best In The Class
22-25	Excellent Student
18-21	Good Student
14-17	Average Student
0-13	Better Luck Next Time

ANSWERS, 2004-05 6th Grade Contest

1. C	9. A	17. C	25. C	33. C
2. A	10. B	18. A	26. B	34. A
3. C	11. C	19. D	27. B	35. D
4. D	12. A	20. C	28. C	36. B
5. D	13. A	21. B	29. A	37. A
6. D	14. B	22. A	30. A	38. C
7. D	15. A	23. D	31. B	39. D
8. C	16. D	24. B	32. D	40. C

RATE YOURSELF!!!
for the 2004-05 6th GRADE CONTEST

Score	Rating
38-40	Another Einstein
35-37	Mathematical Wizard
31-34	School Champion
28-30	Grade Level Champion
25-27	Best In The Class
21-24	Excellent Student
18-20	Good Student
15-17	Average Student
0-14	Better Luck Next Time

ANSWERS, 2005-06 6th Grade Contest

1. A	9. A	17. B	25. C	33. C
2. D	10. D	18. C	26. B	34. A
3. B	11. D	19. C	27. C	35. A
4. C	12. B	20. C	28. A	36. D
5. B	13. B	21. A	29. B	37. D
6. D	14. A	22. D	30. D	38. B
7. C	15. A	23. C	31. D	39. C
8. D	16. B	24. A	32. B	40. B

RATE YOURSELF!!!
for the 2005-06 6th GRADE CONTEST

Score	Rating
37-40	Another Einstein
34-36	Mathematical Wizard
31-33	School Champion
28-30	Grade Level Champion
25-27	Best In The Class
22-24	Excellent Student
19-21	Good Student
16-18	Average Student
0-15	Better Luck Next Time

Math League Contest Books
4th Grade Through High School Levels

Written by Steven R. Conrad and Daniel Flegler, recipients of President Reagan's 1985 Presidential Awards for Excellence in Mathematics Teaching, each book provides schools and students with:

- *Easy-to-use format designed for a 30-minute period*
- *Problems ranging from straightforward to challenging*

Use the form below (or a copy) to order your books

Name: _____

Address: _____

City: _____ State: _____ Zip: _____

(or Province)   (or Postal Code)

Available Titles	# of Copies	Cost
Math Contests—Grades 4, 5, 6	($12.95 each, $15.95 Canadian)	
Volume 1: 1979-80 through 1985-86	_____	_____
Volume 2: 1986-87 through 1990-91	_____	_____
Volume 3: 1991-92 through 1995-96	_____	_____
Volume 4: 1996-97 through 2000-01	_____	_____
Volume 5: 2001-02 through 2005-06	_____	_____
Math Contests—Grades 7 & 8 ‡	‡(Vols. 3,4,5 include Alg. Course I)	
Volume 1: 1977-78 through 1981-82	_____	_____
Volume 2: 1982-83 through 1990-91	_____	_____
Volume 3: 1991-92 through 1995-96	_____	_____
Volume 4: 1996-97 through 2000-01	_____	_____
Volume 5: 2001-02 through 2005-06	_____	_____
Math Contests—High School		
Volume 1: 1977-78 through 1981-82	_____	_____
Volume 2: 1982-83 through 1990-91	_____	_____
Volume 3: 1991-92 through 1995-96	_____	_____
Volume 4: 1996-97 through 2000-01	_____	_____
Volume 5: 2001-02 through 2005-06	_____	_____
Shipping and Handling	$3 ($5 Canadian)	

Please allow 4-6 weeks for delivery Total: $_____

☐ Check or Purchase Order Enclosed; **or**

☐ Visa / MasterCard/Discover # _____

☐ Exp. Date _____ Signature _____

Mail your order with payment to:
Math League Press. PO Box 17, Tenafly, New Jersey USA 07670-0017
or order on the Web at www.mathleague.com

Phone: (201) 568-6328 • Fax: (201) 816-0125